REAL WORLD REAL ESTATE

HOW TO INVEST IN PROPERTY TO LIVE LIFE ON YOUR TERMS

SIMON READ

This book is dedicated to my children, Carter and Grace. You forever make me proud.

It's a big world out there, and I hope this book makes a positive impact in your lives as I have provided a tried, tested and proven roadmap.

First published in 2022 by Simon Read

A catalogue entry for this book is available from the National Library of Australia.

ISBN: 978-1-922764-37-9

Printed in Australia by McPherson's Printing
Project management and text design by Publish Central
Cover design by Pipeline Design

The paper this book is printed on is certified as environmentally friendly.

Contents

Part I
Real world

Introduction

The science of property investing

My property journey

I was 20 years old when I bought my first property. Three years later, I duplicated the process and was able to buy a second. It took another two years to buy a third house, and just a single year after that I bought my fourth. I've used my proven strategy to build a property portfolio that was worth more than $3 million before I turned 30. I've invested in a dozen properties, and sold a few along the way to take some profits, pay down debt, and reinvest in more expensive properties.

The great Australian dream is to own our own home. In fact, it's probably the same dream right across the world: finish school, get a job, save up, buy a house, and in 30 years' time, you're going to be in your 60s or 70s, and you're going to pay that house off, get the title deed and own that property. And then you're going to retire and say to yourself, 'Wow, I've just spent my entire life paying off *one* property, and I have no other income-producing assets?' This is what our parents did; it is what their parents did.

Of course, at 20 years old, who's thinking about real estate? Most people are thinking about cars, dating and having fun. You're not thinking about housing. My friends certainly weren't.

But I was.

There's a publication here in Australia called *Money*, founded and edited by financial planner Paul Clitheroe. When I was young, I had a monthly subscription, and each month I would read that magazine front to back, back to front, many times. It was my bible.

There was a bit of a game I'd play. In the section called 'Ask Paul', people would write in and ask questions such as, 'This is my financial situation, what should I do to get ahead?' Or, 'I'm about to retire and I have no assets, what should I do?' There was a very diverse range of questions and, after a while, I'd consider the question but not immediately read the answer. I got to know Paul's thinking so well that I'd provide my own answer and I'd usually find that he and I were on the same page.

I was fortunate that I had my father in my corner. He advised me at an early age that I would need to buy a house, that having a roof over one's head was a basic necessity in life. My dad's sage advice was, 'The sooner you do it, the better you'll be in the long term.' Nevertheless, it was outside my comfort zone. It was more difficult than it is today. Back then – around the turn of the century – the process consisted of reading the local paper. And those papers didn't have glossy colour photos like you see today. It also involved physically going down to the local real estate agencies and checking in the windows to see what properties they were listing that day.

The internet was around, but it certainly wasn't the internet we know today. First of all, it was slow. Remember dial-up? And people weren't uploading content 24/7 the way they do now. So, to gather information, I did like everyone else: I went to the library, and I'd talk to people I knew.

I soon discovered the first question that needed answering: *what can I afford?* By working a couple of jobs, I'd saved up enough for a deposit. I went to the National Australia Bank and sat down with a bank manager. I wasn't totally sure what I was doing, but I had my dad at my side. After discussing terms, I was pre-approved and now had a working budget.

So, every Saturday – and I mean *every single* Saturday – we would devote the day to looking at houses. I really didn't have much frame of reference, so I didn't have a proper way to contextualise what I was seeing. But over time, I became discriminating. And when I reminded myself that I was going to have to live in one of these places, I became increasingly more particular in what I wanted.

A significant factor for me was that it be low maintenance. I didn't want to spend my weekends gardening. I was still young, and I had plans that didn't allow much time for yard work.

I initially prioritised locations that were near restaurants and shops, where I wanted to spend my time. I didn't really know about the structural side of things, and I had no idea about termites (it so happens that Australia has a massive termite problem). Until then, I hadn't given such matters any thought, but my dad changed that. He would have me consider the proximity of a house to a main road. And while access to a major thoroughfare might be a blessing on one hand, it also meant noise, which could potentially affect future resale value. What I saw as lush greenery along the side of the house, he got me reconsidering as a likely home to creepy crawlies like termites or other vermin.

It was a learning process, and I developed a passion for it. I created lists of 'could haves', 'nice to haves' and 'rather not haves'. I decided on a freestanding, low-set brick-and-tile house with a two-car garage in a quiet neighbourhood near schools, shopping centres and public transport. I found a place that was right, and paid what was then the steep price of $170,000. Since then, however, that property has doubled in value, and doubled again and again.

All those Saturdays spent looking at all those houses was not in vain. On the contrary, I've now been doing this for more than 20 years and the moment I step onto a property, I can begin ticking off the boxes from a 30-point checklist. I'll have a grade on the property within a couple of minutes. It's a process that began with thinking about the pros and cons of every facet of a property, like that nearby major roadway or thick bush on the side of the house. It's a process that is always asking, *where can I add value?*

It's a numbers game

Real estate is very much a numbers game; you've got to go through heaps and heaps of houses before you'll find one right for you. The sooner you can determine that a property doesn't meet your needs, the sooner you can move on to the next one which just might match your criteria. So, it's essential to be able to identify red flags quickly.

When you buy a property to live in, you need to think long term – are you going to be there forever? If the answer is no, which it is for most people, you need to be thinking about how you can resell it in the future and turn a profit. When you select an investment property, you need to keep in the back of your mind that you are not selecting the property for yourself, you're selecting it for the largest number of tenants who are in your key demographic.

The reason you see so many black cars, grey cars and white cars on the road is the resale on those is much higher than, say, a lime green or a purple car. If you're buying a lime green car, do it because *you* want a lime green car, not because you one day plan to sell it. Sure, there may be someone out there who wants that colour, but it's definitely a niche market. You'll have a much easier time unloading a white vehicle, which – let's be honest – no one loves, but no one hates, either. And the person buying your car knows that they'll also have a better chance of selling it when they're done with it.

I'm a very data-driven person. For me, it comes down to facts and figures. I always say, 'the numbers do not lie'. Real estate investing is more science than art. It's about getting the numbers to stack up. If they don't add up, don't buy. It's really that simple.

Getting the right help

We're talking about a huge investment. You're normally buying this piece of property for 10 years or 20 years – maybe even for life. It's not a decision to be taken lightly. In spite of that, I find that so many people go it alone. But they will seek out a mechanic when they need to service their car. When there's a leaking tap, they don't try to fix it themselves, they call a plumber. In other words, in these other, smaller financial decisions, people turn to a professional.

But when it comes to their biggest investment, they often fly solo. They walk into the property and announce, 'I'm going to buy this,' make an offer, and walk out. And it is just mind-blowing that they will use an industry expert for every other aspect of their life, but when it comes to such a life-altering decision they don't seek professional assistance.

Let me take a moment here to distinguish the types of professionals in the field. There are, of course, real estate agents, who are true professionals, but a real estate sales agent is legally bound to look after the *seller's* interests. Their duty is not to the buyer. They will tell you, 'This is the best property for you, it's got three bedrooms, two bathrooms, double garage,' but they probably won't tell you that the road it's on gets really busy during peak hour, or there's an airport a kilometre away and planes fly loudly overhead every half-hour. They won't tell you it's in a flood zone, or that the neighbours play loud music late at night, or that the house has termites.

They're just not going to tell you something negative about the place unless you ask that specific question and they have the information. It's your job to figure that stuff out.

I am a licensed real estate agent and an accredited auctioneer, but I predominantly work as a buyer's agent, so I specialise in assisting people looking to purchase a home or an investment property. I have a passion for helping people, and I've managed hundreds of purchases on behalf of clients. I really feel there's a gap in the market that fails to serve so many people. And they need security; they need a roof over their head, and they need someone to guide them through what can be a difficult and complicated process.

The fact is, you really need someone who has your best interests at heart, somebody who is independent, and someone who genuinely wants to help you buy the right property in the right area for the right price. You don't want to overpay. The seller has someone in their corner, the buyer needs someone as well.

I've gone on to study financial management and business management, and studied elements of accounting, mortgage broking and some commercial law, but only as part of my thirst for knowledge; these weren't taught as a part of a basic high-school education. And, as you've probably discovered, it's those untaught but vital skills that everyone wants to talk about at a barbecue – not maths or grammar. People genuinely want to learn from the conversation. And even a single conversation can honestly change someone's life. I've encountered it countless times.

I have a passion for sharing the knowledge I've acquired. I love helping people get ahead financially. So many people I meet aren't even aware that they're capable of even getting into the market or of tapping into the equity they have to use as a springboard. To be able to present them some options and show them possibilities they had never considered is the best part of my job.

And that's why I'm writing this book. It's to share the information that I've spent the last two decades acquiring so I can help even the folks I'm not fortunate enough to encounter in person. It's my hope that you'll find everything you need in this book to educate yourself with the knowledge to make sound financial decisions in one of the most consequential aspects of your life.

Simon Read
Sunshine Coast, June 2022

Chapter 1

A passive income today leads to financial freedom tomorrow

'If you don't find a way to make money when you sleep, you will work until you die.'

Warren Buffett

The importance of passive income

When extra sources of income don't require your direct time, they are called 'passive income', and they're perfect for bolstering your current salary so you can boost your savings and gain more financial freedom.

What assets do you own *right now*? You may have family heirlooms, or antique furniture, or expensive vehicles and other luxury personal items, and while they do have value, do they also offer you an ongoing income stream? That's something that distinguishes real estate from most other forms of assets.

Investing in real estate that you can then turn around and lease to someone else allows you to earn additional rental income on the side with a minimum of effort. As a bonus, properties increase in value over time, which makes them a worthwhile addition to your portfolio. Real estate has made more millionaires than any other kind of asset.

Here are a handful of very common reasons why it's so important to earn a passive income.

Earning income only from labour

You may be wondering, *I have a stable job, so why do I need passive income?* Everyone works hard these days, and most people have jobs that provide them enough income for their day-to-day lives.

Let's be honest, no matter how much we love the work we do, we are still dreaming of that time when we can finally relax in the knowledge that we're comfortably stable financially.

And here's why you might want to find an additional source of passive income *now*. Jobs that pay by the hour may be regular and stable, but this comes with certain limitations. Once you stop reporting to work, the earning also stops. What if unfortunate circumstances arise? Say you get sick, lose your job or your company goes bankrupt. Do you have a backup plan? Even if you were to find a similar-paying job shortly thereafter, would you be racking up debt in the interim, or depleting your savings?

If you have a passive source of income, you can keep earning during the days that, for whatever reason, you are unable to work. Even while you're enjoying the weekend at home spending quality time with your family, the income flow doesn't stop.

You don't have to be a high-income earner to be wealthy. You just need to take the right action.

Retiring before the government pension age

The Australian Bureau of Statistics has found that while most people intend to retire at age 65, more than half – 55% – of people over the age of 55 in Australia are already retired.

How about you? How do you envision your retirement? Do you want to start the good life at 65 or do you want to be able to sit back and relax while you're still young and have the energy to do so? The real question is, when will you have the financial freedom to do this? The more sources of income you have, the faster you can save up for the retirement of your dreams. And bear in mind, a government pension is not a lifestyle, it's an existence.

Insufficient superannuation

You've probably already thought about your retirement plan. But does your super have enough in it to tick off everything on your bucket list? Is it enough for you to live the comfortable retirement life you so greatly deserve? Remember, the goal is for you to *enjoy* life after retirement, not just simply survive on the super you have worked so hard for. A passive income right now will give you more savings today which you can contribute towards your retirement, and it will provide you with an additional income after you retire.

Doing what you love *now*

But then again, why wait until retirement to start doing the things you love? If you have financial freedom *now*, you'll also have the freedom to make the choices you've always been hesitant to make, like taking more holidays or spending time with the people you love.

> 'You become financially free when your passive income exceeds your expenses.'
>
> T. Harv Eker, author of *Secrets of the Millionaire Mind*

Investing in a passive income source will help you break boundaries, and the best time to do it is now because the sooner you start, the sooner you will begin reaping the rewards, and the greater those rewards will be.

~

If any of the above is resonating with you, it's time to look for additional passive income as soon as possible. The ultimate goal is for you and your family to have financial freedom both today and in the long run.

So, what's the best way to earn passive income? As I'll explain in subsequent chapters, investing in real estate is the most tried-and-true way to generate the most profitable form of passive income. I like to say that if you look after the property for the first five years, it'll look after you for the rest of your life! We're lucky in Australia as real estate offers you so many benefits, including rental income, tax advantages and capital gain over time – so long as you find the right property to get the maximum return on investment.

Chapter 2

Real estate provides the best passive income

'Compound interest is the eighth wonder of the world:
he who understands it, earns it; he who doesn't, pays it.'

Often attributed to Albert Einstein

As we established in chapter 1, earning a passive income is essential for a comfortable life. Unless you're independently wealthy, it's the only way to stop running endlessly on the hamster wheel. To truly gain financial freedom, it's important you have an exit strategy from your day job and find a way to replace that cashflow. There are multiple ways you can do that, so now you may be wondering, *Fine, but why should I invest in* property *to earn that passive income?*

Why property?

There are many reasons why property is the most reliable and time-honoured means of making money while you sleep. And the first is that everyone needs a place to sleep.

Property has tangible value

Because everyone needs a roof over their head, real estate is a commodity that we all require simply by virtue of being human. How many other commodities can you say that about? Unlike the stock market – which we'll look at in a bit – housing has *real, tangible* value. It doesn't just exist on paper. It's made of bricks and mortar … or wood or stone, or steel and … you get the point. At the end of the day, it's something you can physically possess and actually make use of.

Property tends to appreciate reliably

While other investments may fluctuate in value – and wildly, as we'll discuss in the case of stocks – real property not only holds its value, but tends to appreciate reliably. One reason for this, as noted above, is that it's something everyone needs, over generations. And that demand only increases over time as the world's population grows. In addition to that, land is by its very nature a finite resource. As they say, *it's the one thing they're not making more of*.

When you combine those two ideas – *growing demand* and *limited supply* – you don't need a degree in economics to understand that the value of such a commodity is only going to increase. Scarcity drives up the price in any market, whether we're talking about oil or art or property.

The demand for housing almost always tends to be greater than the supply. Why? Well, it's a pretty bad business model to construct houses that aren't currently being sought after in the hope that someday soon there might be interest. Houses – unless they're haunted, or have some major defect – don't sit empty long.

Consider that quote from earlier in the chapter regarding compound growth. When you look at real estate as an asset, you're not just talking about income, you're talking about capital growth. This growth is compounded over time, which means the property is increasing in value by a certain percentage year after year, and it's increasing not on the *initial* value but on the *current* value, whatever that may be after however many surges in value it has already acquired. Roughly speaking, you might expect a well-located property to double in value every 10 years.

You may get a raise at work, but wages are generally not increasing at the same rate as capital growth has averaged over the longer term. If you earn $100,000 from a wage and receive a 5% pay rise, your new income would be $105,000. Now consider a well-located property valued at $600,000 that increased by 5%; the new value is $630,000, an uplift of $30,000. You can see the benefits with real estate – the increase is sixfold over the wages increase.

Here's the other thing about relying on raises at work to achieve your financial goals: they usually come with additional responsibilities. The company isn't just giving away free money; it wants something in return. When you receive something extra in your paycheque, it comes with the understanding that you will now be taking on more duties, putting in extra hours, or just working harder in some fashion or another to 'earn' that bonus cash. In other words, it comes with a price that is paid in additional time or labour in some form.

You may get a standard 3% raise every year for doing the same job, but all that's doing is keeping up with inflation, so in the real world it's not a pay rise at all.

Property is inflation-proof

Property rental amounts *rise* with inflation, which increases your cashflow. And increased cashflow is a nice thing to have during an inflationary period. Additionally, there is likely to be an influx of renters who enter the market if mortgages become too costly with a rise in interest rates. Both are win–win situations for you as a property holder.

It should be noted as well that rising inflation and interest rate hikes are inevitable economic cycles, not rare once-in-a-generation events. Holding property is an effective hedge against downturns, and an investment that thrives in both good times and bad.

Property has tax benefits

I don't want to get lost in the weeds discussing the particulars of tax law, but suffice to say, there are a few major tax advantages you are able to access when you invest in property, such as negative gearing and tax deductions on mortgage interest, holding expenses, insurance and depreciation.

Now, I don't advise investing in property to lose money, and I make every effort to ensure my clients choose only those properties that are most likely to appreciate in value, but that said, it is helpful to know there are tax deductions available that can assist with cashflow and ultimately help you on your investment journey.

It's entirely legal – and wise – to take steps to protect your wealth and pay less taxes.

Why *now*?

There's a saying I live by:

> 'Don't wait to buy property; buy property and wait.'

Procrastinating about buying a property is costing you. You may have been told that everything comes to you at the perfect time. But often, waiting for that 'ideal' moment can also result in missing some great opportunities, and never is this truer than when it comes to buying property. In fact, there are a variety of ways in which waiting for the right time bears a hefty price tag. And while you may think that holding off will save you from entering the market at the wrong time, chances are you're preventing yourself from reaping all the benefits it provides as well.

In my experience, people procrastinate about buying a property for a variety of reasons. But they all result in the same problem: *inaction*.

The reality is, the Australian property market naturally goes through regular cycles, seasons and trends, all of which take values up and down. This uncertainty can make first-time buyers and seasoned investors alike feel a little worried. After all, the idea is to buy low and sell high. Naturally, you want to enter the market as the tide is rising rather than receding.

Nor does it help that media focus tends to be on the bad news rather than the good, confusing potential buyers, especially when they hear that fluctuations in the interest rate are 'going to lead to a disaster' or that the property bubble is 'predicted to burst' soon. But doom-and-gloom forecasts are, of course, what drives the news.

Such worry and confusion can transform into a paralysing fear which understandably affects potential buyers and holds them back while they wait in constant anticipation for a future in which things are better.

This can actually be a costly mistake.

Truth is, there is no such thing as perfect timing when it comes to investing, and nobody can accurately predict the market's next move. All that we can say with a level of certainty is that the market tends to level out into a state of equilibrium, meaning you should strike when you're ready.

In the end, having a property today means it's working for you *now* with all of its potential benefits, as opposed to waiting for a property to come along sometime in the future; and as opposed to that property providing its benefits to someone else, who went ahead and made the investment.

As discussed above, those benefits begin with earning a passive income. They also include holding in your portfolio an investment that carries tangible value, appreciates steadily, withstands inflation and thrives with interest-rate hikes, and also provides tax benefits.

The best time to invest was *earlier than today*, but since that ship has sailed, the next best time is *now*. The worst time is *later*.

The bottom line is, I hear from so many people as they look back over the years and say, 'I wish I had bought earlier'. To which I feel like replying, 'I wish I could've been there to help'. This book is an attempt to be there to help so that the next person who might have been paralysed into inaction will have the confidence to take that bold leap forward.

Real estate vs the stock market

You're ready to invest, and you want to get the best return on that investment and you want to reduce risk as much as possible. So, why should you buy property, as opposed to putting your money into shares? Let's examine the main differences between the two.

Speculation vs ownership

As discussed above, residential real estate is a basic need of life all around the world. So, housing is capable of maintaining its value despite economic shakeups such as the Global Financial Crisis or the COVID-19 pandemic. In fact, when a catastrophic event does strike, the first thing many people do is sell their shares. They try to liquidate positions to get cash in their hands quickly.

Real estate, however, is not something you buy and sell every day. Nobody day-trades in housing. You don't hold onto your ANZ stock but sell your house – it's the other way around. Shares are a luxury, while housing is a necessity. Generally speaking, people will do whatever they can to protect the roof over their head.

I'm not suggesting your portfolio shouldn't be diversified – it absolutely should be – but understand that the stock market is by its nature a much more volatile environment than property, and part of the reason lies in the differences between being a speculator and an owner. Buying shares in a company is not the same as buying a home. Those shares can be bought and sold, then bought and sold again and again, with only a small trading fee as an impediment. Shares are traded second by second, and the market fluctuates daily (hourly, really), going up and down like a yo-yo.

The housing market functions much more slowly and deliberately. Of course, it can rise and fall too, but you will not see the same volatility that can infect the sharemarket. For one thing, a property transaction is much more procedural, involving large holding deposits, lengthy contracts and third parties (in most instances). Buying a house requires on-site inspections, building due diligence, looking for evidence of termites, and dozens and dozens of other hands-on forms of research. If you want to buy shares in Apple, you can go online and look over the financials, or listen to the quarterly earnings reports, or maybe get a hot tip from your broker, but the company isn't going to have you over to inspect the next design of the iPhone.

Most investors simply hold shares until they're ready to liquidate them for cash. When a home is sold, usually there are real-world consequences that follow. People uproot their lives to move from one place to another, taking their worldly possessions with them. Again, this is the difference between a person who is speculating about whether a kind of mobile phone is going to outperform market expectations and a person who is purchasing a home on a piece of land in a neighbourhood where they will raise their kids. That person has much more skin in the game, and that level of commitment reduces volatility.

The banks know this, of course. Try getting a loan to buy some shares. It's certainly not like getting a loan to buy a house. The minute those shares drop in value, you may get a knock at your door and be told you need to repay the money you borrowed, and right away – as in, *today*. And if they fall further, you may get another knock on the door tomorrow. That's just not the case if the housing market dips. I've never heard of a situation in which someone bought an investment property that dipped in value and had the bank show up and demand immediate loan repayment.

Property is stable. It's tried, tested and proven.

Property provides control and the ability to add value

One of the most critical distinguishing factors between property and shares is the ability you have as a property owner to increase the value of your investment. A simple cosmetic refresh – new paint on the walls, new carpeting, add LED lights, provide some natural lighting, switch out the kitchen benchtops, spruce up the garden – can immediately boost the value of your piece of property.

That said, I don't necessarily advise major overhauls on an investment property. The addition of a swimming pool, for instance, is an expense that doesn't necessarily equate to a proportionate upgrade in value. Some potential buyers may look at that pool as an additional expense, requiring regular upkeep, higher electricity usage and the occasional maintenance fee. The same could be said of many so-called upgrades, which in fact do not offer much return on investment, and might even diminish the allure of the property to the key demographic you're trying to reach.

The point is, you really can bolster the value of your investment with inexpensive, cosmetic improvements. And that's all under your control as an owner.

Now, compare that to your role as a shareholder in a company. Unless you own a significant – and perhaps controlling – percentage of a company, you have little or no say in what that company does on any given day. What they do is entirely up to their own discretion. You can't improve it no matter what you do.

And by extension, neither can you do anything to prevent the company from behaving in a manner or making decisions that negatively affect your investment. If that company's CEO makes a boneheaded move and the stock price tanks, there's nothing you can do about it but take the loss. It's out of your hands. Voting for change at the next AGM will be too late.

So, in the case of property, you can take matters into your own hands and make improvements that can *increase* the value of your investment. And in the case of shares, your investment is in someone else's hands, which could actually result in actions that *decrease* the value of your investment that you can do nothing about.

Property provides leveraging potential

Borrowing is an essential component of wealth-building. As they say, *it takes money to make money*. Consider how long it would take to buy even an inexpensive parcel of land with cash. And here's the problem with that: while you're saving up that money, the land keeps increasing in value – or in your case as a potential buyer, in cost. If you already owned the land, you would be reaping the benefits of its appreciation, rather than paying for it in your eventual purchase.

Property appreciates faster than the interest you're collecting from your bank account, and more reliably than your shares. You want to own it as soon as you're able, which usually means taking out a loan to get it. The interest on the loan is rather negligible relative to the appreciation of the real estate. So, if you're going to invest in property, you're naturally going to borrow the bank's money to do it.

The bank has no problem with that. Banks see residential properties as an extremely safe investment for their part. They're willing to front you money as collateral on it: this is *leveraging*. If you want to get a loan based on your shares, that's going to be a very different conversation because it's a much more risky investment on the bank's part. If your shares fall for whatever reason, the bank may demand a 'margin call', meaning you're going to have to sell some or all of those shares at a substantially reduced value to repay your loan. And to circle back to the idea that you have no control over a company's actions, you've now really put yourself in a risky situation. That's a scenario you simply don't have to worry about when you're in control of the thing being invested in.

Chapter 3

Setting up your property team

Who's who in the zoo

The average family buys a home once every 10 years. There is no way you can be an expert at something you do only once every decade. Buying a property is not something you do on your own. It involves a team of professionals all working together to achieve the ultimate goal of settling a property.

Just as important as choosing the right property is choosing the right *people*. You might just find your dream home and be ready to buy it and move in, but if you've chosen a dodgy someone in one of the supporting roles, it could undermine the entire purchase. That's why I only work with the best. I want experts in their jobs who have years of experience, who are there for me when I want to talk, and who I can trust to behave ethically and responsibly.

That is going to cost a little bit more, and that's fine. There are cheaper options out there, but why take chances on such a large investment? Is it really worth it? Sure, you might save a little money up front, but if someone you've hired in this process overlooked or half-assed something, there's a good chance you're going to pay for it later, probably when you least expect it, and probably at a much higher price than if the thing had been done correctly in the first place.

Keep that in mind as you consider the following list of professionals. These are the people who can help make your property-buying experience a seamless operation, or a disaster. It's important to understand the duties of each and to make sure you have the right person in each role.

Buyer's agents

Searching for the right property takes time and effort. It requires internet research, setting up inspections, and driving all over to view properties every week. It will take a toll on even the hardiest among us. If you've been through the process, you have no doubt wondered if there was someone who could help you; someone who does this every day and has the institutional memory, industry knowledge and track record of experience to make the best decisions.

In fact, there is. That person is a *buyer's agent*.

Also known as a *buyer's advocate*, this person is a real estate professional who helps buyers find the best available property at the best possible price.

Acting on your behalf, the buyer's agent must not only be equipped with a real estate license, but also the know-how and negotiation skills necessary to satisfactorily represent your interests as a property investor or homebuyer.

The buyer's agent is in a certain way the opposite of a real estate sales agent, as they are serving opposing parties: buyer and seller, respectively. Each agent has a fiduciary duty to their client, and as such can be considered trustworthy, as their ability to practice their profession is directly linked to their behaving ethically.

The role of the buyer's agent will be examined at length as part of the next chapter, Understanding the buying process.

Mortgage brokers

A mortgage broker can make or break the entire transaction. That's why this is usually the first person I go to when I begin the buying process. To be specific, it's important to find an *independent* mortgage broker. An independent broker is there to service the customer, and doesn't work for the bank. A bank-employed mortgage broker's first allegiance is to their employer, the bank. An independent broker has a duty to the bank as well, but primarily to the customer.

When you deal directly with a bank, you have to understand they have a certain way of doing things and you're just going to have to accept that. For example, they tend to work from 9 a.m. till 4 p.m. Ever try to reach a bank after hours? How did that go? You've got to fit into the box that the bank gives you.

I'll share with you a little secret. The big banks really don't care about their clients – at least, not their existing ones (okay, maybe that's not such a secret after all!). They want *new* customers. To that end, they offer cheap interest rates, but only to lure customers away from other banks or to attract people who do not yet have a bank. And it does make sense in a way. If you're an existing customer, are you really going to leave? Are you going to start out with another bank that you don't really know or trust? At the very least, it sure is a hassle.

Another model, which the banks *could* follow if they so chose, would involve providing top-notch service for existing clients in the knowledge that those clients would in turn refer their friends and neighbours, thereby bringing in new customers through positive word of mouth.

But that's not how banks tend to operate, as I'm sure you know.

An independent mortgage broker, by contrast, is generally self-employed or running their own small business. To remain competitive they must provide quality service, and to do that they will generally meet with you in person, take your calls after hours, and often go the extra mile for you and offer next-level service.

An independent mortgage broker would have access to all the products that the bank has, but they'll have multiple banks on their panel. We have four big banks in Australia, and they might each have 12 or 15 loan products and options. If you go to an independent broker, they are likely to have those same products, but by also having access to a panel of other lenders, they might have anywhere between 30 and 50 loan products to compare, to choose the best deal for *you*. Given this broader range of available options, you are ultimately going to get a much better product.

It should also be noted that each bank has its own slightly different lending criteria. You might not fit neatly into the box of the particular bank you usually go to, and you might get rejected as a result. But if you go to a broker, they will run all your information – income, liabilities and everything else – through their lending software and find out where you best fit.

Generally speaking, mortgage brokers are paid by the lender. So, they get paid when the deal settles. Naturally, they really want to do their best to make sure that the financing comes together. In that spirit, they quite often follow up with the client to ensure there are no missing documents, they will make sure everything is compiled properly, and ensure that there is a proper briefing report put together. Ultimately, you have a better chance of being approved.

And if you're worried that maybe the broker would unscrupulously recommend a lender in some sort of 'kickback' arrangement for a commission, keep in mind that you are entitled to find out *why* a lender has been recommended. At the end of the day, the broker is going to have to explain the reasoning behind the recommendation. It's a regulated industry, and such shady business practices are just not worth it for the broker. The potential consequences are too dire.

If you go directly to a bank, you're dealing with an employee. They do not have the same incentive to get you approved because it's not *their* business. That person is paid a regular salary for their time – whether or not a deal is closed. Because of that, they often really don't connect with the client. That's not to say that there aren't exceptions – people who genuinely care about buyers and go out of their way to be helpful – but are you going to gamble on that?

I want to work with someone who has skin in the game – a person who has a vested interest in getting me across the finish line with the best lender. That might mean finding the cheapest interest rates, or the lowest fees and charges, or the one that can get your pre-approval ready in half the time.

As you can see, a broker plays an important role in making sure the finance is done on time with the best lender. In fact, that's why I went and completed a Diploma of Finance and Mortgage Broking. It has provided me with insights into exactly what is involved in the broker's process.

To briefly summarise, it's customer service that distinguishes an independent mortgage broker. If you go to a mortgage broker, you have a better chance of getting your loan approved, rather than going to a single lender. It's also more likely to be approved more quickly and to be the most ideal product available to you. And 12 months later – after the bank has moved on – you will probably receive a congratulatory follow-up on the anniversary of your loan settling, and a reminder that if you need anything, the mortgage broker is just a call away.

Building and pest inspectors

You've purchased a beautiful four-bedroom house with a white picket fence in a charming neighbourhood with great schools and a delightful shopping centre nearby. You should be happy. You should be focused on pruning your roses, cutting your lawn, and buying groceries and goods, but because you didn't follow through with your due diligence, you are having to spend thousands of dollars replacing leaky pipes or repairing termite-damaged walls. Overnight, your Australian dream has become a nightmare.

This is why I tell my clients that a building and pest inspection is compulsory. It is simply part and parcel of proper due diligence. It's non-negotiable.

Building and pest inspectors examine the physical health of the residence. They check to ensure there are no structural problems. The go into all rooms, climb up on the roof, rummage through the attic, peek into every nook and cranny. Often, they will discover cosmetic faults as well, things which could potentially cost you a lot of money to fix down the road.

These are professionals who know what they're looking for. Would *you* be able to determine the moisture levels in the walls, for instance? If you happen to carry a moisture meter reader around with you, well, good for you, because this is an issue that arises all too frequently.

I bought a house a couple of years ago that was only five or six years old. It was rather stylish, freshly painted and presented quite nicely. I wasn't expecting that anything could possibly be wrong with it. Of course, I put into the contract my standard due diligence clause that provides for a building and pest inspection, just to be thorough. Sure enough, upon inspection of the primary bathroom, the moisture meter readings were through the roof. But to the naked eye, everything looked perfect.

The readings were not even coming from anywhere near the shower, where you might expect there to be a waterproofing membrane that had busted, causing water to penetrate into the wall. So, with the owner's consent, we performed an invasive inspection, drilling a hole through the plasterboard and putting a camera in there to see what was going on.

What we found was that in fact it *was* the shower's waterproof membrane, and it had failed because it was not installed properly. The water had been getting into the wall cavity and travelling through the wall. The damage wasn't behind the wall of the shower itself, but rather it was about four meters away.

Needless to say, I went back to the seller and renegotiated the terms of the deal, requiring the issue be repaired to a professional standard.

By including the building and pest inspection clause in the contract, I provided myself the ability to nullify the deal if the seller opted not to fix the problem. As it turned out, the seller did fix the problem and I wasn't stuck with the bill. That bill, by the way, was $7,500.

That problem could have been even worse, and probably would've become much worse if we had not discovered it when we did. Wet timber is not just a structural problem, it's also a potential pest problem because it promotes termites. Termites love wet, damp areas, so if you have a bathroom that has moist or wet wooden posts in the walls, that is going to attract termites, and they are going to feast. And once the termites are in your house, they don't just eat and run – they go everywhere.

That's where the pest inspector comes in. This is a separate person from the building inspector, and is an expert in vermin, and they make sure that the house is free of these little creepy crawlies. Australia has a variety of termites and wood borers.

The pest inspector will conduct visual inspections, looking everywhere including the roof and even using thermal-imaging cameras to see beyond what ordinary eyes are capable of uncovering, spying into the walls and other cavities. They will even poke around the boundaries, looking for trees and shrubs that could be housing termite nests. I've seen countless properties where there's a rotting old stump or a pile of wood chips in the yard – and they are loaded with termites. Now, that in itself is not a dealbreaker, but you want to make sure that they're exterminated right away, before they go looking for something else to chew.

Recently, I have seen a lot of people buying property online – without even visiting the place. Maybe nothing will go wrong, but that's a real roll of the dice. Why would you blindfold yourself when you don't have to? Do you think the seller's agent is going to announce the faults of the property? Do you think they are going to bring up the fact that you would probably never know it from the look of it, but the house is actually located in a flood zone? That agent is trying to get the highest possible return for the seller, not lower the asking price. The seller's agent has a fiduciary obligation to the seller, but not to the buyer.

That house I purchased with the moisture damage that was coming from the shower? The seller wasn't trying to slip one by me – he wasn't even aware of it. It hadn't given him any trouble, and wasn't even visible. A building or pest problem doesn't usually show up immediately; it could be weeks, months, or even years later – perhaps when you are trying to sell the property yourself – that the damage is ultimately discovered.

A building and a pest inspection requires a professional in each of those fields. I have reviewed hundreds and hundreds of inspection reports, I know a lot of the telltale signs and I am pretty good at spotting potential hazards, but I would never even consider forgoing the expertise of a professional. They are definitely worth the price.

Bottom line, if you're not willing to do your due diligence, you can't complain when you find out there is a major problem that they would have uncovered.

Conveyancers

A conveyancer is a property law specialist who deals with all aspects of buying and selling. They will review the contract, check the terms and conditions, and make sure it's all compliant with relevant legislation. They will also organise your council searches, checks and balances, rate searches, and basically manage the relationship between the seller and the buyer until settlement. That means they will also liaise with the banks to make sure there is enough money ready for settlement.

I like to work with a conveyancer who will take my phone calls anytime, day or night, who has been through enough settlements to know the exact process, and who understands where things can get derailed.

In recent years, a lot of new businesses have been popping up which offer conveyancing. It has become very hands-off and electronic. You plug everything into the platform on the internet and it works out the details. And that's great when everything goes according to plan. But what happens when it doesn't? That's when you want someone with the expertise to know what to do and to take action fast. Maybe the seller has filed for bankruptcy, or a council search flagged the property saying there are problems with a building approval – there is a wide range of issues that can arise.

We rely so heavily on the internet now, but it can be a crutch that keeps us from looking a little harder to find the *right* tool for the job rather than the most *convenient* one. A conveyancer is someone worth having a professional relationship with, rather than a one-off transaction. Because of that, I rely on the same conveyancer in each state, as property law differs from state to state. So, when I'm purchasing a property in Queensland, I have a go-to conveyancer to get that deal done.

And if something goes wrong along the way? I get on the phone directly with that person and they know just what to do. If you are using a conveyancing business you found online? Well, you have to go back online and enter some information into a form, it runs through a workflow process, and the wheels go into motion.

You don't get any extra level of service, any explanation, any assurances like, 'Don't worry, Simon … I've handled this situation before a hundred times and I've got it under control. I'll give you a call this evening.'

Quite often, property purchases – particularly residential properties – run like clockwork. But there will always be hiccups along the way. It might be finance documents that have not been done properly, or the council has not processed something *just so*, an *'i'* hasn't been dotted or a *'t'* crossed.

There are several parties ultimately involved, so there are a lot of touchpoints, and it could be any one of a range of things that go wrong. If or when it does, it can cause a delay to your settlement, or the deal could fall over all together. So by having the right conveyancer on your team, you will make sure that the deal you've worked so hard to put together actually settles in the end.

As a practical matter, one of the areas where I find things tend to fall apart is the communication process between conveyancer and buyer. Some important piece of information is not relayed in time or explained sufficiently enough for the buyer to understand the urgency of a matter, and as a result, a key deadline is missed.

A great deal of property transactions don't settle on time for one reason or another. If you have agreed on a certain settlement date, and if you don't meet that timeline, you can seek an extension from the seller. However, the seller can then charge you interest *payable daily* for any extra time that you would like, plus penalty fees to cover any additional expenses, so it can become very expensive if you have to extend settlement.

Now, if the buyer has a strong relationship with the conveyancer and they have worked together before, it's logical to assume that there would be better lines of communication, and those delays could have been avoided. Furthermore, it's important to understand that the solicitors are not paying those fees, so if a settlement period is extended, it's no skin off their nose. But if the two of you have a good working relationship, it's safe to think they would go out of their way to spare you those extra expenses.

Another point at which deals fall through is when a conveyancer does not have the necessary experience to handle a problem, or isn't proactive enough to head off a potential pitfall before it arises.

Your conveyancer should not be the weak link in your chain. Consider how much money and effort you're putting into your property purchase. Are you really going to cut corners here and simply pull a name out of a hat or take your chances with a Google search? Do so at your own risk.

Insurers

Insurance is another non-negotiable. The lender requires itself to be listed on the policy as the mortgagee, so you can neither progress nor convert your pre-approval to a full approval, then have the loan settle *unless* you have appropriate insurance.

I will recommend a certain insurer to my clients based on the high-level service they provide, as well as the level of coverage. Part of the decision depends on whether you're buying a property to live in or to invest in. If it's an investment property, you need to have *two* lots of insurance: you need to have building insurance to cover the physical structure, and you need to have landlord insurance to make sure that if anything happens with the tenancy, you're covered for malicious damage, rental defaults and other such contingencies. Those are two separate policies, but it's very important to have both.

Often, a client will prefer to use their own insurer because they have a good relationship with them, or if they've got multiple policies they may qualify for discounts, which is perfectly fine. Each insurance company has its pros and cons and different levels of coverage, so it's important for people to compare insurance companies apples for apples to make sure they are getting the identical level of coverage and the same premiums, and to ensure that any excesses are the same.

Because it's outside my area of expertise, I can't really give insurance advice as such, but it is super important that the right level of insurance is taken out. So, what I do is take it a step further and I look at online calculators, for instance, where you can calculate the rebuilding costs properly.

With all the videos and photos we have on file of any property that I intend to buy, I will go back through and review those with all the other data and information we have on a property. I insert all of that content into the calculator to work out the proper rebuilding costs, to make sure we're using accurate figures.

If you happen to underinsure your property, yes, you'll save some money each year on your premium, but if anything untoward does in fact happen, you are going to have to build with a shortfall of funds you recover from your unsatisfactory insurance policy. With that in mind, if anything, you're best to slightly overinsure your property to make sure you really do have enough coverage. And then you need to review that annually.

Some insurance companies are much like banks, in that you might get discounts for the first couple years after taking out a policy. But after that, the discounts disappear, and the premiums go up. The reason for that, generally speaking, is that when people take out insurance policies, they simply tend to renew them year after year without giving it too much thought. Insurance companies know that, of course, so they feel comfortable in raising premiums or otherwise adjusting policies in their favour. Not only should you be reviewing your policy every 12 months, but you need to compare it with similar policies from other companies to make sure you are getting the best value for your money.

The same thing goes for your home or investment loan. You ought to review it every two or three years to make sure there isn't a better loan product out there that you are missing out on. New lenders often try to pull in more business by offering deals to new customers. If you do in fact discover a better deal, you can either take it or you can go back to your current lender and ask them if they would be willing to match the offer. Most banks will match the offer. They don't like taking the chance of losing a customer.

Insurance companies operate the same way. If you have a relationship with them, they can, sometimes, offer discounts if you let them know you are going to leave for one of their competitors. Most insurance companies have a customer retention department that can authorise a 'customer loyalty discount' or something of that nature as a way of keeping your business.

The insurance company is not going to *offer* you a new deal, but if you do the legwork to find the better deal, they will usually play ball. By doing that little amount of research, you can use the information you acquire as leverage to obtain a better deal one way or the other.

Accountants

There are accountants, and then there are *accountants*. The difference between a good accountant and a great accountant can be summed up in a word: *proactive*. You want someone who knows the tax law so well that they can bump right up next to the line without ever crossing it. This is a person who understands how to use the tax code to your advantage, actively searching for write-offs and loopholes.

A great accountant understands how to use a depreciation schedule to free up your cashflow position, which you might use to invest in your next property. There are a lot of production line accountants out there who follow the law. You want to have an accountant who *uses* the law. The best accountants cost more money, but it's money well spent because it's money that will eventually make its way back into your pocket.

You may remember billionaire Kerry Packer some 30 years ago being grilled by the Senate about his extremely modest tax bill. His reply was something to the effect of, 'You'd have to be stupid to be paying more tax than you have to.' That was a man with very proactive accountants who knew exactly what you could and could not claim.

Talk to your accountant. Ask questions. Have conversations about your goals and your options, the same way you would talk to a financial planner. Make sure they're not just annually processing your tax return, but that they're being continually proactive on your behalf.

Property managers

Most of my clients understand the value of the professionals listed above. Those are jobs that are clearly best left to experts in their respective fields. But where I tend to find that a client feels bold enough to go it on their own is in the role of property manager. Let me be clear: I don't recommend this.

Let's dive in.

Is hiring a property manager better than self-management?

As an industry professional, I naturally encourage property investment for all the reasons discussed, particularly the passive income. However, for real estate to begin providing that steady flow of reliable rental profits, you first need to lease out the home. And when you do that, you need to decide whether you are going to hire a professional to manage the property or whether you're going to do it yourself.

So, what does property management entail? Here is a brief list of just some of the primary tasks required in managing a rental home:

- advertising your property to attract tenants
- preparing the lease documents
- screening all potential tenants
- collecting rent regularly
- managing general upkeep and maintenance
- legal compliance and enforcement
- checking in on tenants' needs
- finding and screening new tenants when vacancies occur.

Are you ready to take on all those responsibilities, even as you work towards and search for your next investment property? Do you feel comfortable calling up the tenant because they haven't cut the grass, or they put up a sign in the yard that some neighbours find offensive? Can you do that without making it personal or emotional? A property manager would treat it like business … because for them, it *is*.

The advantages of hiring a property manager

Property managers are a team of leasing and rental agents – typically part of a local real estate agency – who handle the day-to-day operations of your property on your behalf as the landlord. Not only do they help with tenants and sort out all the administrative aspects, but they make certain that your investment goals are met by offering you their experience and in-depth familiarity with the industry.

So, why should you entrust your investment to a property manager?

- *Time*

  Simply put, property managers save you a great deal of time. I listed a handful of required duties above, most of which demand a lot of time and attention. A property manager dedicates their days to undertaking those responsibilities, freeing you of the burden. Recall the reasons why you sought a passive income in the first place; wasn't part of it to find more enjoyment in life?

- *Better returns*

  Property managers generate larger returns in rental income. In leasing a property, you are trying to achieve optimal cashflow and maximum income. To do so requires setting rental prices and managing expenses. Given their knowledge of the market, property managers are highly qualified at setting competitive rental prices to attract quality tenants, implement an effective rent-collection system, and manage countless transactions such as monthly expenses, regular maintenance and emergency repairs. Getting those details right ensures the maximum return on your investment.

- *Legal expertise*

  Australia has numerous laws and legal procedures in the field of real estate. Every state has its own set of rental and leasing laws that must be abided by, and most property managers are well-versed in the laws of their particular state, and understanding rules, regulations and practices. The consequences of being out of compliance can be extremely burdensome and ultimately quite costly.

- *Knowledge and experience*

  The greatest advantage property managers provide is a wealth of knowledge gained over their years of managing properties. They have learned how to create the most efficient systems, adequately address tenant needs, answer questions and deal professionally with any issues that arise.

- *Peace of mind*

  When you hire a quality property manager, you can trust that they will consult with you on important decisions and provide timely updates to keep you in the loop. They filter out the particulars, so that you can focus on the big-picture issues.

The advantages of self-management

Of course, some investors find benefits in managing their property themselves, such as:

- *Savings*

  This is the primary reason that an investor chooses self-management of a rental property. After all, property managers, while generally not being too expensive, do require service fees.

- *Greater control*

  Being your own manager means having total control over your property. All the decisions and requirements – from the leasing to the screening to record-keeping to maintenance – are in your control.

- *Experience*

  If you're committed to putting a lot of hours into real estate, learning how to run your own systems might be considered a thing of value. And by maintaining your independence, you're bound to gain experience … likely for the better *and* the worse.

While these benefits may sound appealing, it's also important to consider the non-financial facets such as handling tenant complaints, or an unfamiliarity with the range of local property laws, and of course, the time and effort required.

So, after considering both sides of the equation, should you hire a property manager? I suggest the answer is yes. Let a reliable property management company take care of your investment, so you can focus on growing your wealth.

As a professional in the industry, my goal is to help my clients buy the ideal investment property as a way to add wealth, income and other benefits to their portfolio. That needs to be followed up with effective leasing, and that's where a good property manager is indispensable.

A common misperception is that property management is rather simple. In fact, it's a lot more complex than it appears. It involves performing routine inspections, dealing with bond lodgement, and managing maintenance and upkeep. Furthermore, handling tenancy legislation can be a minefield that could very well put you at risk. Trying to deal with tenant matters is generally a tedious process. Remember that while it may be an *investment* to you, it's a *home* to them.

Here is a little insight into my process for finding a property management company. I begin by checking into the number of properties a company has in its portfolio. Is it a few dozen or 600? What's their workload like? If you've got a small team of two or three property managers and they're managing thousands of properties, you've got to expect the quality of their work to diminish because they are stretched too thin.

Then there are questions you must ask to find out how they handle various situations. For instance, what happens if someone does not pay rent or is often late paying? Or what if there are complaints from neighbours? Or what if tenants damage the property? Go through some scenarios with each property manager and determine how each would respond to an array of potential pitfalls.

Once you find a few acceptable options, it boils down to negotiation. For me, because I buy multiple properties, I want to establish relationships with these property managers, so for example, I may offer volume in exchange for a discount that can be passed on to my clients. Most importantly, I want to work with a property manager with a sense of ethics, someone who will look after the property as if it was their own.

Quantity surveyors

A quantity surveyor is strictly for investment properties. They are able to prepare a depreciation schedule so that you can collect any tax benefits you're due as a result of a loss of value to the property. Buildings sustain wear and tear over time. Paint fades, tiles chip, doors are damaged, and so on, and so on. These are examples of depreciation.

Australia has a lot of rules regarding the claims that can and can't be made. Recent legislation allows the owner to claim building construction costs, but for existing houses, you can't claim the fittings and fixtures until such time that they break and are replaced. A quantity surveyor will be familiar with distinctions like that.

In essence, a quantity surveyor determines the lifetime of everything within a property. If the building is going to last 40 years, they will work out the life expectancy of the dishwasher, the carpets, the blinds – everything – and figure out what you can claim each year as a tax deduction. It's the job of a specialist – it absolutely needs to be done by a qualified professional who is registered with the ATO.

Depreciation is a valuable tool for managing cashflow. It is imperative to take advantage of every tax deduction you are eligible for.

Part II
Real estate

Chapter 4

Understanding the buying process

Four ways to buy real estate

There are generally four ways in which people will buy real estate. Let's take a look.

Private treaty

This is a process in which you browse advertised homes, and make an offer on ones you like based on the listed price. You then negotiate with the vendor or their real estate agent until you reach a satisfactory price for both parties. At the time of contract signing, there is generally a 10% deposit required.

There is a cooling-off period which allows a purchaser to change their mind and withdraw from a contract; the timeframe for the cooling-off period varies between states and territories. If you decide to walk away and exercise this right, there is typically a financial penalty equivalent to 0.20% to 0.25% of the final sale price of the property. You should seek legal advice before cancelling a contract.

This is the traditional homebuying method.

Auction

An auction is a one-off event. You register as a bidder, and compete with others on auction day – whoever has the highest bid over the set reserve price becomes the new owner of the property.

A vendor bid can be used to start an auction or to get the bids moving closer to the amount the seller is willing to accept; these vendor bids can only be made by the auctioneer and must be announced to the bidders. The number of vendor bids allowed varies from state to state: in New South Wales the vendor can have one bid, whereas in Tasmania vendor bids are unlimited. Buyers can feel uneasy with this process since the seller is competing directly with the buyers to push the price up.

It's important to know that in Australia, there is no cooling-off period for property purchases made at an auction – if you're the winning bidder, that's it. There's no turning back, so make sure your finances are in order *before* you bid.

Tender

With the tender process, there is not necessarily a listed price. You submit an offer along with a 5% or 10% deposit, and the vendor will accept or reject this depending on whether it meets their wants and needs.

Off the plan

This is a method of buying in which you actually make the purchase before the property is built. Usually this is done by engaging developers or their representatives, and when finished the property can look slightly different than that which was advertised.

Off-the-plan purchases can be appealing for buyers who like the certainty of having a fixed-price contract and the peace of mind knowing the property will be built at a later stage; however, it has become more common for builders to issue their clients with expensive contract variations; this could be for any amount of money – $30,000 to $90,000 isn't unusual. This can happen at any time. It could be before the build starts or close to completion.

The reasons for a contract variation might include increases in the cost of materials and labour, or a desire for a higher profit margin. It's a hard pill to swallow given a buyer signs a fixed-price contract, and the situation could become a nightmare for people if they don't have access to extra funds. If the construction has not commenced, they might consider their options to cancel the contract.

It's crucial to scrutinise the inclusions list so you know with certainty what is actually included; such as, what kind of lighting will be included, LED downlights or just conventional light bulbs with no decorative covers; likewise, bathrooms and laundries need adequate ventilation, therefore will exhaust fans be installed in all bathrooms and the laundry?

Another common item that can be overlooked is the landscaping. Often the brochure for the property will include words like 'fully landscaped' or 'turnkey package', however in the fine print it will include that the block must not exceed a precise area, say 450sqm, and if your land size is larger, when the landscaping is due, the builder will either ask for more money or only complete the bare minimum requirement and then hand over the property for you to complete what's outstanding.

The timeframe to build often gets blown out by months, so make sure you have a contingency plan.

Also, don't overlook having a legal review done on the build contract and ask your lawyer to explain any sunset clauses. A sunset clause puts conditions and limits on the contract, and depending on the wording, could let you, the builder or the developer cancel the contract. In a strongly rising market, a developer could be tempted to cancel a contract to then resell the property for a higher price – this is unethical but it does happen.

Seven tips on the buying process

Tip 1: Determine your expectations

Before you jump feet-first into investing, it's important to work out what your expectations are. For starters, that means determining exactly what your budget is. When I talk to my clients, the first thing I want to know is the amount of available funds that are set aside for the investment.

It's important to establish a buffer so you don't overcommit yourself and end up overburdening your finances. If you don't have the extra cash at the end of the month to meet up with friends or go out for a nice dinner, you probably should reconsider your budget so as to be realistic about how much disposable income is accessible for discretionary spending.

Bills and other expenses hit at different times during the month, and during the year. Have a look not only at your monthly expenditures but at your annual expenditures as well. You need to make sure you're not overextending yourself so you can buy within your means. This is a process that requires a lot of honesty with yourself. You don't want to live a frugal life while you're waiting for your investment to eventually pay dividends.

Tip 2: Plan far ahead

I'm always looking 10, 20, or in some cases 30 years out for my clients. When do they want to retire? What kind of passive income are they striving to achieve? Do they own their own residence, or is there a way to pay it off ahead of schedule?

Real estate by its nature is a long-term game. I don't believe in buying and flipping (selling again quickly to try to make a quick profit). It's not like buying and selling shares. You're paying too much in the initial purchase price in stamp duties, legal fees, and due diligence. When you sell, you're paying a selling agent. The transactional costs involved are simply prohibitive. Ideally, you want to hold a property for at least 10 years, but the longer, the better.

I've got clients who want to buy three or four properties over the next 10 or 15 years. We begin with one property and start generating passive income and eventually purchase a second property. Those properties not only pull in rents but also increase in value, and now the client is able to tap into that equity and slowly build a portfolio from compound growth. And it begins to snowball until, at some point, the first three properties begin paying for the fourth.

Eventually, you get to a place where the whole portfolio is *positive* cashflow. And that cashflow is a supplement to your income that can either fund your lifestyle or begin paying the principal on the loans down.

Tip 3: Have an emergency fund

With many years of experience, I have developed a rule of thumb. I recommend having at least $5,000 set aside as a safety net, which you're not tapping into on a regular basis. It's there just in case a hot water system breaks or the air conditioning malfunctions, and you're stuck with a one-off expense that requires urgent payment.

Or, what if a tenant vacates a property and you experience a period in which there's no rent coming in? Or – and it's not the sort of thing you want to think about – what if someone in your life got sick or lost their job or got into some kind of a jam that required your help?

Having a cushion of at least $5,000 in an offset account gives you the peace of mind to know that if or when one of these unexpected problems arises, you're ready to handle it. Consider it an emergency fund.

Tip 4: Examine your loan options

There are a range of options if you're in the market for a loan. You want to do your research to find your best option, and then have it examined by an independent mortgage broker who will help you align the loan with your goals and timelines.

There are a lot of banks out there, and each has dozens of types of loan products with varying interest rates, monthly fees and establishment fees. Some have credit cards, some allow you to pay the mortgage back ahead of schedule, some have offset accounts.

You need to determine your ultimate goal. How many properties are you looking to buy? You need to set up the initial loans based on what you plan to do down the road. It's a strategic game plan that needs a lot of upfront thought. You can always refinance your loans, but it is an inconvenience and there will be costs. Good planning can spare you some time and trouble in the future.

As we previously discussed, you don't want to go directly to a bank. They are going to show you what *they* have, which may or may not be the best loan product available for you. They aren't going to tell you that a competitor down the street has a product that is much more in line with what you're looking for. An independent mortgage broker can show you *all* your options.

Tip 5: Decide on principal or interest-only repayments

When you have your initial consultation with your independent mortgage broker, they'll help you figure out which loan products are best for your particular situation. One of the key items to work out is whether the loan will have principal-and-interest or interest-only repayments. The answer to that question aligns closely with whatever your particular goals and aspirations are. How many properties do you want to buy? At what price? Will it be owner-occupied or an investment?

Take that last question, for instance. Let's say this is your dream home and you're living in it and you want to pay it off. Your best bet would be a principal-and-interest repayment plan, as the interest payments are not tax deductible for a primary residence. And if it's not a tax deduction, you definitely want to pay down the principal as quickly as possible. Whereas if it was an investment property, you might want to pay interest only, as it would be tax deductible, while you hammer away at the principal on your main residence. If something is tax-effective, you want to use that to your advantage. So, you would want to pay off your main residence as quickly as you can.

Additionally, you will generally find that the interest-only payments on an investment property are less burdensome. Why? Because you're *only* paying interest, not the principal as well.

Consider what that might look like in terms of your investment property. If you were looking at, say, $2,000 a month in principal-and-interest payments, you might only pay $1,200 monthly in interest-only payments. That $800 you're not paying on the principal of your investment property can instead be used to pay down the principal on your primary residence which, again, is not tax deductible.

Or, you could take that $800 a month and roll it into funding a *new* investment property – or shares or bonds or whatever else you choose to get ahead financially. I'll say it again: use the tax code effectively to your advantage.

Tip 6: Budget for interest rate increases

Interest rates change over time – they're not a constant. They go up, they go down. In fact, they change fairly regularly. And each lender may offer their own slightly different rate. Rates may be low when you get your loan, but expect that figure to rise. You should always factor in at least two to three points above what you're currently paying just as a precautionary measure.

There's nothing worse than buying a property when rates are exceptionally low and basing your lifestyle and further expenses on that rate, only to have it go up. If you haven't prepared for the increase, you're going to have to find a way to cover the difference. Maybe that means taking on a second job or maybe it means having to sell the property because you can no longer afford it.

Whatever the case, it's a situation you never want to put yourself in. And on the bright side, if rates don't go up, that's great news. You've got a surplus of cash and a buffer for the future.

Tip 7: Select the ideal property

When you are buying your main residence, there are a lot of factors that must be considered. There are lifestyle factors, for starters. You probably want to live in a blue-chip area that is close to the city or the beach, or to wherever it is that you enjoy spending time. You are buying it based not solely on facts and figures, but on your emotional connection. It's not a business decision like with an investment property. It's the place you will call *home*.

But, if it's an investment property you're looking to buy, that's a different story. And one reason for that is you are not just buying it for yourself, you are buying it for your prospective tenant. You will need someone who wants to live there. What does *that person* want?

You're selecting a property for which you think you can get the best return on your investment. In my experience, that's a house in an area that is either established or growing. The average renter – and that's most likely who you're trying to attract, rather than a small niche of potential tenants – wants a low-maintenance freestanding house on a separate block of land that is big enough to have a small dog or a trampoline in the backyard.

And that makes sense. Who wants to spend their weekends doing maintenance or work on a house they don't even own? One of the greatest benefits of renting is you get to enjoy your lifestyle and have someone else repair or maintain the property. It is one of the perks that renters enjoy, which makes the deal more attractive on their end. Some people, even property owners, prefer living in a rental property for its ease and simplicity.

It's important to look at the data when you're considering investing in a property. Who is the largest demographic you're aiming to attract? Is it a family of four with a dog and a cat, who wants to host barbecues in the backyard? Is it a busy business executive who is always on the go? Or is it a retired couple whose children have grown up and moved out? They're all likely going to want something different. So, you need to know who is going to want to move into your property.

You never want your property sitting vacant week after week. So, that means finding a property that is similar to those around it. Not the cheapest house on the street, which will probably be empty until every other house is occupied, nor the most expensive, which could be vacated by the tenant in the event of a financial burden. You don't want *unique*, as that is going to turn some people off; remember, you're looking for the *largest* demographic.

Buy the right kind of property in the right area and don't overpay. Okay, but what's the *right* kind of property? To begin with, it's something that doesn't require a lot of upkeep. If it's in a family-friendly suburb, it ought to have a yard large enough to have neighbourhood children over to play, or to host friends for a barbeque, or a place for the dog to do its business. It should be near a grocery store and schools. It should be away from train tracks and not under a flight path. It should simply be on par with the homes around it.

In any area, most renters are looking for the same qualities in a home. In a suburb, maybe it's four bedrooms and a yard; by the beach, maybe it's a patio with an ocean view; in the city, maybe it's proximity to cafes, restaurants, pubs and shops.

The point is, whatever the neighbourhood, there is a *largest* demographic of potential renters that is on the market for a certain list of 'things' in a home. Your job is to find out what those things are, because that's what you as a landlord are striving to provide.

Estimating a home's value

Before diving into the guidelines for determining the value of a residential property, I feel it's worth addressing a new trend that has recently been emerging in the market. This is a subject that is near and dear to my heart because I work with buyers, and whether it's a sophisticated investor looking to expand an already-impressive portfolio or a young couple hoping to find their first home, they're not industry professionals. There is no reason for them to be steeped in the latest nuances and intricacies of the real estate business. When I act as a buyer's agent, I have a duty to protect their interests and make sure they don't overpay.

So, I have grown concerned lately by the number of properties that are being sold without an advertised price. I get a ton of emails these days that provide a set date of sale and 'invite offers'. Would you buy anything else that way? Of course not. You wouldn't go into a clothing store and buy a pair of socks that way. Why would you make your most important and costly purchase in such a haphazard way?

So, why would the selling agent not put a price on the property? What they've apparently discovered is that they don't actually have to. The housing market represents uncharted waters for a lot of buyers and they don't know how to accurately gauge the worth of the property. They wind up entering into bidding wars against other buyers who are just as uncertain of the value as they are. Every buyer offering a bid feels stressed out from the process and doesn't want to miss out on a home they're ready to buy.

The tactic can be quite frustrating to buyers who might think they have a legitimate shot at the house, only to discover it is actually selling for much, much higher than anticipated. What happens is that they are often given an attractive estimate, but the truth is, that number is just a carrot being dangled in front of them to get them in the door. Because the more potential interest in a place, naturally, the greater demand … and the higher the eventual price.

With that in mind, it is more important now than ever to accurately estimate the worth of a property. And that's where a real estate agent comes in. We have ways to calculate fair market value. But first, let's define the term.

Fair market value

Fair market value (FMV) in real estate is the price that a property will sell for in an open market. The FMV is agreed upon between a willing buyer and seller, both of whom are reasonably knowledgeable about the property in question.

Implied within that definition is the idea that the seller is not in some way distressed and desperate to sell, even at a reduced cost. The FMV is a number agreed upon by both buyer and seller after all the relevant research has been done.

Comparative market analysis

When a seller lists a property for sale, the selling agent must provide a comparative market analysis (CMA) to 'prove' the worth of the listed property. It's the selling agent's task since the seller is not usually a real estate professional and they need guidance with setting a realistic advertised price. They also need to understand how the selling agent estimated the price. On the other side of the equation, the buyer generally would not know what factors to consider, much less have the tools or the skills or the software.

That said, the buyer will want a CMA, too. Without one, you would be left to simply accept the figure given by the seller's agent rather than taking the opportunity to argue for a lower fair market value. Again, that is where a buyer's agent is invaluable. The buyer's agent will formulate a separate CMA conducive to, obviously, the buyer.

A CMA involves establishing a few parameters as you study at least three similar properties that have been sold. And it is important to identify properties that have *actually* sold, not just those that have been listed on the market.* The reason, of course, is that a listing price is most likely not the final price for which the property will be sold. A listed price will in all likelihood skew results in the seller's favour.

A CMA takes into account many factors, including:

- *How far away is the comparable sale?*

  Ideally, you want to find a similar property that has sold within a relatively close distance, say five kilometres. Anything farther away than that is really not a true comparable.

- *How recently was it sold?*

  The data needs to be rather fresh, as the market is always in a state of flux. Six months is about as far back as you can go before the selling price is no longer relevant.

- *How long was it on the market?*

  How many days did it take from being listed to being sold? In other words, is it a hot or cold market? Scarcity and high demand will increase the value of a property. The difference between three days on the market and 23 days can ultimately be measured in dollars.

- *What is the land size?*

  Once you account for location, you need to consider the size of the piece of property. Again, you want to be comparing apples to apples so you can properly gauge the value. If you're measuring two vastly different properties in terms of size, you just aren't going to get a fair equivalent.

---

* These settled sales can be sourced from *CoreLogic* (formerly *RP Data*) or real estate websites.

But then, size isn't everything. Suppose you have a 40-acre backyard filled with waist-high weeds. It may also be filled with vermin of one kind or another. Land of this nature is more of a liability than an asset, and is going to require the new owner to pay to landscape it.

- *What is the block like?*

  Even if the land size is equal, there are more questions to ask – for example, is the block sloping? Or is it a flat block? Is the land usable? How is it zoned? Low density? Medium density? High density? Multi-use or strictly residential?

  Furthermore, the orientation matters. Is it a north- or south-facing block? Does it get morning or afternoon sun? Does it get a lot of wind relative to its neighbours?

  Or, take it a step further … if it's in a beach area, is it ocean-facing or inland-facing? Is there anything blocking a view?

- *What is the home age and condition?*

  How old is the structure? Does it have the normal wear and tear of just being lived in or are there damages that go beyond that? Are they cosmetic blemishes or are there structural or internal defects that may cause serious problems down the line?

- *What is the home size?*

  Is the home of similar proportions to those around it? If it's much smaller than those around it, are your tenants going to want to entertain neighbours, or will they always have to pay visits? And if the home is a lot bigger than the comparable homes in the area, it's important to ask why. Was it overbuilt? Are you overpaying for space that your tenants may not need or use?

- *What about beds and baths?*

  How many bedrooms are there? One? Two? *Five?* Are they tiny or roomy? Bedrooms can limit how many children a family might consider having. Additionally, the number of bathrooms may well limit the number of guests that one might invite over. Are guests going to have access to a private bathroom, or will they have to use the children's bathroom – or trounce through the master bedroom to the en suite?

- *Does it have additional living areas or a media room?*

  Most modern homes are designed to provide comfortable living space to enjoy playing games or watching movies. A formal space for receiving guests is a traditional feature of the home, but more than ever a relaxed setting to spend downtime with the family has become a high priority among homebuyers.

- *Does it have air conditioning (ducted or split system)?*

  In Australia, all houses should have air conditioning. Nevertheless, some don't. But that's not the end of the situation … some have *ducted* air conditioning, in which the system reaches all the bedrooms and living areas. It is *ducted* into those areas. And then there is what is known as a *split system*, in which you usually have one or two smaller units that provide cooling for their own specific areas.

  Two properties that are otherwise indistinguishable can be vastly different in terms of the quality of comfort they provide based only on the type of air conditioning system. A ducted system could run up to $20,000, while a split system might only set you back about $3,000. That's enough of a differential to affect the overall cost of the property.

- *Does it have a solar system?*

  Where does the electricity on the property come from? Is it supplied or do you want to generate it yourself? A basic solar system might cost you about $10,000. Then again, you could end up spending as much as $30,000 if you went top of the line, and that needs to be factored in as well.

- *Does it have a pool?*

  A pool could increase the cost of a property anywhere from $50,000 to $100,000. And if you are comparing a house *with a pool* to one *without* a pool, you need to factor that in. If all the homes on the block have a pool and the one you're looking at doesn't, it's not really a genuine comparable, and that difference needs to be added into the equation.

- *What about the kitchen?*

  The kitchen is the heart of the home. You eat there almost every day for breakfast, lunch and dinner. That's where you have your conversations. It is where you're making your meals and where everyone congregates. That's where life – and the memories we have – really happens.

- *Other factors*

  Sometimes, a home may appear comparable on the surface, but if you dig deeper, you realise that something is off. Maybe a neighbouring home sold for the same price, but has two more bedrooms and bathrooms, and a pool. And after you look into it, you find out that it was sold to a family member. It was parents selling the house to one of their children, and they wanted to give them a deal. That's not a good comparable.

  Other times, you may find out that the owner recently died and that the heirs just want to sell the property and divide up the money with as little fuss as possible. Or maybe someone is in dire financial straits and needs to liquidate all assets in a hurry.

  It is also the case that homes sell above market value, and for a variety of reasons. Perhaps it was sold at auction, and the bidder – probably stressed out from the buying process and desperately wanting to be done with it – got too caught up in winning the auction and overpaid. I have also seen cases in which a buyer has a strong emotional attachment to a property – maybe it was a childhood home – and considered it invaluable.

The sales agent may list such homes as comparables, and unless you do your due diligence to uncover these distinguishing factors, you might just accept that they *are* comparables and end up overpaying.

Negotiating your property purchase

Everything is negotiable. What I mean is, like most things, there is a level of influence you can exert on an outcome – and real estate is no different. Bear in mind, however, that the process of property negotiation is not always simple.

Once you've found the property you want to buy and you've done your due diligence to determine the fair market value, the next step is to negotiate the price. Now, if you have not found the appropriate comparables, your estimate of the home's worth is going to be off to some degree or another, with the result that you will have a significant blind spot about the actual value, and so you will be negotiating from a place of weakness.

There is no such thing as a price tag on a house. Every property deal is open for discussion. If you accept the seller's initial price, you will almost certainly overpay. Reaching the final figure, the number at which the home ultimately will sell for, is really a bit of a dance. The selling agent understands the choreography: a price is announced, a counteroffer is proposed, and back and forth, and this for that, and cha cha cha.

Aiming for a win–win situation

But remember there's a lot more that is being negotiated than just the price. That would essentially be a zero-sum game in which one side wins and the other loses, depending on whether the selling price was above or below actual fair market value.

You have no doubt heard the old adage, 'You can't have your cake and eat it, too.' This is a principle that is often applicable to a negotiation scenario. Of course, you can't just give in to the seller's desires to close the sale. But you also can't expect the seller to do the same for you, either. Keep in mind that while you may be trying to get a hefty discount, the seller – unless it's a quick liquidation-type situation – is going to be looking to get a little something extra in the profit column.

A good negotiation involves concessions of factors you might not necessarily value but which the other person does, and other factors for which they're willing to make concessions of their own to make the deal more alluring to you. For example, I've seen negotiations in which the seller has pushed for a higher price, and being on the buyer's side, we've accepted but only on the proviso that a border fence is replaced before settlement, or some other form of critical (and likely expensive) maintenance is accomplished.

A negotiation is about finding a *win–win* scenario. Done correctly, both sides can walk away having enjoyed the experience and being happy with the result.

What is the seller's motivation?

Every buyer knows what constitutes a win for their own part, but understanding what the seller would consider a win requires knowing what motivations are behind the desire to sell. In other words, *why* are they selling the property?

Are they looking at a quick settlement or a long settlement? Do they have another place to live already lined up or are they planning to go house hunting? Do they want rent-back provisions? What could you do that would sweeten the deal?

Knowing the seller's motives is a crucial part of the negotiation process. Maybe the sale is financially driven following a divorce, bankruptcy or major financial loss. Maybe the sale is motivated by a traumatic event such as a recent death in the family, or it could be that the seller is just thinking of upgrading or downsizing.

Whatever the case may be, these factors all need to be considered as they affect the seller's rationale in the negotiating process. And if you are aware of those considerations, you will be able to make more informed decisions on your end.

But finding out what that motivation is can be a dicey proposition, to say the least. Asking why someone is selling their home is always a touchy subject. On top of that, the selling agent has a duty to the client and is tasked with certain confidentialities. That said, they can often work in their client's best interest by empowering you, the buyer, with some explanations or details which might be conducive to reaching a win–win deal.

I'm not suggesting anything untoward, mind you; I'm just saying that sometimes, merely casually offering a friendly compliment about the home can yield some helpful insights: 'What a lovely house, I can't imagine why anyone would want to sell such a beautiful place … ' It's just being … diplomatic.

Keeping emotion under control

Buying a property, especially one in which you intend to reside, is a serious decision which carries with it a lot of emotions that can cloud your better judgment and obstruct logical reasoning. The buying process is stressful, it has long-lasting consequences, and requires about 10,000 decisions in various sizes from inconsequential to life-altering.

With so much at stake, it's not hard to understand why buyers sometimes go a little nuts in the heat of the moment and bid a bit beyond their means because maybe they've grown really attached to a place, or maybe they don't like their other options, or maybe they're just so tired of the whole ordeal they just want it to be over.

If you want to fully leverage your negotiating power when buying a property, it is imperative to keep your cool and remove the emotional element from the process. That is a lot easier said than done, I realise, given that buying a home is either a part of your investment strategy or it's a major life goal. But the negotiation process can't be emotionally charged because it involves thousands of hard-earned dollars and time, which both you and the seller have invested and wish to make the most of.

Once you have come to accept that negotiations are not to be taken personally, and that it is at its core a rational exchange of benefits and concessions, it becomes easier to maintain control of all those emotions.

And once you have excluded the emotional aspects of the venture, you are ready to focus on some of the finer points of the negotiating process.

The bottom line

The bottom line is there is a lot of time and effort that goes into working out what a property is worth. It's a ton of research to determine fair market value, but given enough datapoints, it's an equation that can be solved to a pretty accurate degree. And if there's going to be a lender involved, you can be sure they are also going to send in a qualified property valuer to provide their estimate of the home's value. You better believe that if their analysis is you are asking for money and it doesn't look like a very good deal, they are not going to sign off on a loan.

If you don't know the fair market value, you are more than likely going to overpay for a property. But, on the other hand, if you have a buyer's agent on your side who's done your homework for you, when you are ready to enter into the negotiation process you'll go in with your eyes wide open.

Seven tips to get the best negotiation outcome

To help you negotiate the best possible outcomes, I have developed a list of seven tips that I've learned over the years as a buyer's agent.

Tip 1: Cash is king

Money talks. If you're using cash to fund a purchase, any seller will be more confident about the sale and will take you more seriously as a buyer. You can leverage this, of course, to your advantage. All else being equal, a cash buyer is preferable to one who requires a loan, which comes with the inherent possibility of the deal falling over.

Having cash in hand can also speed up a deal, which could be a thing of value to a seller. Even if a buyer is pre-approved for a loan, which is an absolute must, circumstances can change – maybe you changed jobs since the pre-approval, or you aren't in the same financial position as before, or maybe the lending guidelines have been updated. And if that's the case, there's nothing that guarantees a pre-approved loan will be converted to an unconditional loan approval.

If you are a cash buyer, you want to announce that with a loudspeaker. Don't be shy.

Tip 2: Don't start small

If you start with an offer that is too low, you just might offend the seller, and that may be the end of your negotiation. So, start with a reasonable purchase price and work from there.

I have seen it myself – a buyer either can't afford the property or wants to lowball the seller to try to get a better deal and ends up going in with a ridiculous offer. And if that seller isn't distressed financially, but might be a bit house proud, it's going to be a problem. That home is their baby, they've put their blood, sweat and tears into it. They have spent years living in it and made special memories that they will always cherish.

So what happens when some stranger comes along and essentially says the home is worth much less than the owner thinks by making an insulting offer? They're going to take it a little personally. And they're going to tell that buyer to take a hike. Things get off on the wrong foot, and there's just no getting back on track.

You can't start small. The owners know the value of their home and you're likely either going to insult them or make them think you haven't done your due diligence to determine the fair market value. Either way, it's hard to recover from such a rocky start.

Tip 3: It's not always about the money

It's important to see the big picture. What is motivating the seller? There may be other factors the seller considers to be of great value. If you can work with that, you may be able to adjust the selling price accordingly. By being flexible and responsive to the other party's needs, you may be able to get something you value in return, which might be a price reduction or it might be some other form of compensation you write into the contract.

Essentially, if you give a thing of value, you can get a thing of value in return. And if it costs you nothing to do so, why wouldn't you?

Tip 4: Great deals take time

Don't rush the process. Be flexible on the settlement date, so the seller doesn't become frustrated or agitated, as this generally only leads to more difficult pushback. Nobody likes to be backed into a corner or receive an ultimatum, like, 'make a decision now or I'm just going to walk away'.

Everyone makes decisions based on their own experiences and in their own manner. Some people need to be able to assess whatever it is you're offering and fully digest it before coming to a conclusion. If you rush that person's process, you are probably dissolving the whole deal.

In any financial arrangement of this magnitude, paranoia can run high, and a seller being hurried might think, 'What's the rush … am I asking too little? Did I not do enough due diligence in trying to determine the fair market value? Is this buyer truly legitimate, or perhaps if I did a little more probing I might discover something that should cause me concern?'

Again, knowing the seller's motivation will give you really good insight into how you should conduct the negotiations. It could well be the case that a seller is highly motivated to move things quickly along. It could be a family who has already bought their next property, for example, and they may well want a quick deal. They might say, 'Let's make this happen. Let's sign off on this today.' They don't want to risk a longer settlement because then they're going to require bridging finance for their next property.

Knowing that's their situation would allow you to negotiate using their desire to rush the process as a bargaining chip. You might agree to hurry things along if they agree to come down a little on the price. If that means they avoid having to go through the bridging loan route, they would probably see that as a win. And with that, you have the best-case scenario: a win–win.

Tip 5: Give them options

Options can help smooth over some conditions and ultimately secure a better outcome. To return to an example, it could come in the form of a rent-back option for a short period to give the seller more time to find their next property. Having a roof over their heads and the peace of mind that comes with being able to make an informed decision about their next home purchase is presumably something a couple selling a house would place a high value on.

It would also ensure that your property is not sitting vacant. You have an immediate tenant from day one. Win–win.

One proviso, however … If you were buying the property with the intention of having it as your primary residence, you would not want to offer a rent-back with an indefinite time frame. There is stamp duty to be aware of. If you are not living in the place for six months to a whole year, then you're technically an investor. As such, you will pay more stamp duty. That's just a caveat to keep in mind.

Tip 6: Know when to walk away

It's important to recognise a bad deal when you see one and to have the courage to turn your back on it. That means knowing the limit you're willing to go to. Certainly that's the case with regards to price, but you also need to draw some boundaries with other aspects of a deal.

If a six-month settlement period is longer than makes sense for you, walk away. If they're not willing to let you do the necessary inspections, consider that a red flag. Know what is negotiable and what is non-negotiable. And if it doesn't stack up and make good commercial sense, you just need to move forward and look for other opportunities.

This is particularly important for buyers at auctions, where emotions can run hot. Egos often get involved, as nobody likes to lose what is basically a contest, and in such a public setting. Add to that, you have an auctioneer who is orchestrating those emotions like a symphony conductor, and you have a recipe for prices getting way ahead of where they ought to be.

And this is where Tip 7 comes into play …

Tip 7: Bring an expert in to help you

The key benefit of using an agent as your proxy is that it removes all the emotion. When I bid for a client, I know what constitutes a good deal and what my client's budget is, and if the price of a property rises above that level, I don't get caught up in the moment, I'm not overly attached to the house, my ego isn't involved at all. As a result, I can simply stop bidding and know that I've done right by my buyer. And the same holds true in a normal negotiation on a private treaty sale.

The average family buys a home once every 10 years; there is simply no way you can have anything approaching expertise when you only do it once a decade. And especially not when you are up against a trained sales agent who does this for a living. It's not a fair fight.

When it comes to something as significant as purchasing property, you want to have an experienced buyer's agent by your side. We negotiate real estate every single day and know what to look out for. We know what you can and can't do, or what you might bring to the table to tip a deal in your favour.

We have your best interests at heart and will ensure you secure the best deal.

How to purchase with confidence

So now that you know a bit more about the process and how it works, how do you get ahead of the pack and purchase with confidence? Every year, new laws are written governing property, meanwhile markets are constantly adjusting, and new players enter the industry even as old ones say farewell. This happens in every state. Keeping abreast of the ever-changing landscape is literally a full-time job. It's *my* full-time job. I'm a real estate agent, and

I monitor everything that happens in this domain for my clients because there simply is no way a property buyer who works outside the industry can possibly be an expert in this field.

A buyer's agent can make all the difference in finding the perfect property and guiding you through the process from *once upon a time* to *happily ever after*. But there are a lot of buyer's agents in the market, with varying degrees of expertise and offering a range of services. With that in mind, it's important for potential buyers to educate themselves in order to find the right agent for their particular needs.

The buyer's agent aims to make the buying process as smooth and easy as possible. They strive to eliminate the stress and hassle of the real estate transaction while helping the buyer make thoughtful, informed – and profitable – decisions. How? The following are the services that a quality buyer's agent will provide:

- *Searching properties in areas with strong growth potential*

  A buyer's agent scouts for properties with your given criteria in mind. With their expertise and experience, this person uses their knowledge of the market to find ideal investments with a lot of potential for return.

- *Performing inspections of properties*

  A buyer's agent attends multiple property inspections and open homes on behalf of buyers like you. That spares you the time and expense of trying to gather that information yourself. They also use their professional insights and objectivity to assess each home's suitability, then report back to you.

  A buyer's agent who has a wide network may even provide you with access to properties not yet on the market, allowing you to consider properties before they are even advertised for sale to the public.

- *Participating in auction bidding*

  Smart auction bidding requires a set of tactics, knowledge of the market, hands-on experience and strong negotiation skills. Having a professional buyer's agent handle the process on your behalf will give you a much better chance of securing a property at the best possible price.

- *Asking the right questions and obtaining the necessary information*

  You can't ask what you don't know. And to take that a step further, you're not even aware of what you don't know. A buyer's agent, on the other hand, will know what questions to ask and how to get the correct information when dealing with real estate agents. This will ensure you are fully equipped to make an informed investment decision.

~

Now that you know more about what buyer's agents do and the benefits they offer you, the next step is to pick the right one for *you* because not all buyer's agents are the same. Many who claim to be experts may in fact lack the necessary experience or qualifications to adequately represent a buyer. That's true in most professions though – there are some good ones and some not-so-good ones.

If you are not careful in your decision-making, you could hire a buyer's agent who does not customise a search for properties that are right for your circumstances, leading you towards a less-than-ideal buying situation.

So, how do you find the buyer's agent who is right for you? Here are six important questions to ask of a buyer's agent:

- *Are you fully licensed in the right locations?*

  It's one thing to be fully licensed, but it's another thing to be licensed in the right place. Each state and territory in Australia has its own real estate licensing requirements. If the buyer's agent you're considering is licensed in Victoria but you're looking to buy in Queensland, that's going to be a problem.

- *Are you a member of any governing industry body for real estate agents and property professionals?*

  Being an approved member of a governing industry body ensures that the buyer's agent is bound by a constitution and accountable to a professional code of conduct. Ethical behaviour is essential in this business, and a rogue agent acting on your behalf can scuttle your current deal and damage your reputation, making it difficult for you the next time you attempt to buy.

  In addition, other professionals are much more likely to interact favourably with someone who is endorsed by a respected organisation. After all, people working in the same industry are likely to encounter each other again and again. If your buyer's agent is known for operating in *good faith*, it will reflect in your buying experience.

- *Do you have a financial interest in any properties for sale?*

  It's important to know whether they have a financial interest in a property they are presenting to you. By asking this question, you can steer clear of someone with a conflict of interest who is just acting as a salesperson. An exclusive buyer's agent will act solely on your behalf and not prompt you to buy one of their investments from a partnered builder who is providing an incentive to make a sale.

- *Will you be physically inspecting the property?*

  Make it perfectly clear that on-site, in-person inspection of the property is a necessity, and that mere internet research is insufficient. After all, you could just go online and look into it yourself without having to involve anyone else.

- *Do you have a track record that's backed up by client testimonials?*

  Gaining the insights that have been provided by previous clients will ensure you aren't just throwing darts blindly at a board to make a selection. It's helpful to know that your buyer's agent has completed numerous successful transactions before. Property buying is a complex field with a lot of moving pieces, and there is a great deal of knowledge required that only comes with experience. It's completely fine to ask for references. And be ready to follow through with researching your buyer's agent.

- *What services do you offer?*

  Is your buyer's agent offering a full property search? On-site inspection? Or just auction bidding? Whether it's only one transaction or the spectrum of services from initial search to negotiations to dotting the proverbial *i*'s and crossing the *t*'s, you need to know what you are expecting by involving a buyer's agent.

In fact, let's shed some light on the relationship between buyer and buyer's agent.

What is your involvement with a buyer's agent?

Simply put, a buyer's agent does *everything* for you. Relying on their real estate knowledge, industry networks and negotiating abilities, they represent you and remove most of the legwork and tediousness from the purchasing process, enabling you to buy smarter.

So, what do *you* do? Simple: you sign and initial a whole lot of documents. That, and you actually pay for the property. Lest we overlook that tiny detail.

The process requires a strong working relationship. A good buyer's agent will keep you in the loop as much or as little as you desire, and at every important milestone, involve and educate you about what's going on and what it means in practical terms.

To give you a sense of what your involvement might look like, consider a typical start-to-finish process in the purchase of a property:

1. *Initial consultation*

   Before you engage your buyer's agent, you'll begin with a chat about your goals and preferences, your budget and your requirements. This will help the person better understand what you're looking for and determine if you would make a good match.

   The buyer's agent will then tell you about their services and provide you with a Buyers Agency Agreement. And once the agreement is signed and the engagement fee is paid, work can immediately commence.

2. *Finance pre-approval letter*

   Before getting too serious about research and negotiations, you must provide a copy of your finance pre-approval letter from your lender to your buyer's agent. If you don't have a trusted mortgage broker, your agent can offer suggestions on where to obtain a mortgage. Finance is an important step towards purchasing a property and it needs to be done absolutely right.

3. *Research phase*

   This is the stage in which your buyer's agent will start searching for ideal property locations and homes around Australia that fit within your requirements and budget. This includes online research, of course, but also calling real estate agents and inspecting properties in person.

   This step spares you the numerous days you would have spent personally scouting the market.

4. *Negotiation*

   Now, your buyer's agent will speak to the selling agents and engage in discussions on price. You can simply sit back and rely on their expertise and let them do all the hard work of getting you the best possible deal.

5. *Contract of sale*

   Once agreement has been reached – which includes the price, settlement date and other key terms of the contract – the buyer's agent will arrange for the Contract of Sale to be prepared.

6. *Property presentation*

   The buyer's agent will now present you with the selected property and their research in addition to their rationale behind the choice. They will also present the Contract of Sale to sign, while offering guidance and answering any questions.

   This is the part of the process where you come back in. You'll be asked to review the property and discuss your thoughts with your agent to come to a decision to purchase and move on to the next step.

   If you do decide to proceed with the purchase, make sure you return the Contract of Sale as soon as possible, because until the contract has been signed by both buyer *and* seller, it is not binding and the seller can change their mind and sell it to someone else.

7. *Holding deposit*

   Your buyer's agent will give you the details for the real estate agent's account so you can place your initial deposit.

8. *Solicitor or conveyancer's contact*

   Your buyer's agent will liaise with a solicitor and/or conveyancer who will work on reviewing all the legal processes and documentation. Fortunately, you can rely on your buyer's agent to have a wide network of legal professionals who can provide these services at the best price. This way, it's all arranged for you.

9. *Building and pest inspections*

   Your buyer's agent will ensure your property undergoes quality building and pest inspections. They will source the right service providers for you and review the reports to check for any potential issues. They will then raise any concerns with you and, based on your level of satisfaction with the results of the inspections, organise any further negotiations with the seller if required.

10. *Written approval*

    Once you've reviewed the reports and are satisfied, you must provide written approval to the seller's solicitor that confirms you are satisfied and the purchase can proceed to settlement. Your agent will be able to assist you and provide guidance on this.

11. *Insurance policy*

    Your buyer's agent can provide you with guidance and suggestions about insurance requirements, including building and landlord insurance. As you certainly don't want to take chances, it's important to ensure you're covered.

12. *Property management paperwork*

    If you are planning to lease, your buyer's agent will search locally and negotiate with property management agents to find the best option for you.

13. *Depreciation schedule*

    A depreciation schedule is a document that tells your accountant how much depreciation you can claim on your investment property. A buyer's agent can help you organise this too.

14. *Final inspection*

    Your buyer's agent will conduct a final inspection before you settle, just to ensure that the home is still in the same condition as it was when first inspected. A little time will have passed since that initial inspection, and you want to be certain that nothing has changed in the interim.

15. *Settlement*

    Your buyer's agent will liaise with the conveyancers/settlement agents and confirm when settlement has been completed. They will then ensure that you receive all the documentation you need.

Congratulations, it's now time to sit back and let capital growth do the heavy lifting for you!

~

As you can see, a buyer's agent will transform the whole property-buying process at every stage from stressful to convenient. Because I'm quite familiar with the process after two decades in it, I think of it as a symphony orchestra, in which my role is that of the conductor.

Chapter 5

Residential vs commercial property

When it comes to property investing, there are a lot of options out there. Choosing the one that is right for you can provide stability in the form of a passive rental income as you work to grow your wealth. Real estate is also a tangible asset that tends to accrue value on its own over time, while also offering potential tax benefits and leverageable equity. But of course, the question is: *which kind of property is right for you?*

There are essentially two types of property you can purchase: *residential* and *commercial*. To this point I've been discussing residential property, as housing is a basic commodity and will always be in demand. In addition, you can add value to a dwelling by adding improvements and making renovations. There are also the tax deductions and exemptions, and the ability to leverage equity to create borrowing power. Let's now consider the pros and cons involved in investing in commercial property.

I want to begin by saying that a well-balanced portfolio includes both residential *and* commercial properties. It's not an *either/or*.

But if you're just starting out or are considering where the bulk of your investment dollars should be positioned, this chapter will make a case that as lucrative as commercial properties may be, they are a much more complex, volatile and ultimately unreliable revenue generator than residential properties.

What is commercial property?

A commercial property is any structure used to conduct business or other form of activity associated with industry or commerce. Examples range from shop fronts to offices to warehouses to factories. In general, such properties offer higher gross rental returns than their residential counterparts.

Commercial properties that cater to profit-generating activities come in a variety of forms. The three most popular are:

- *Retail:* Stores, shops, restaurants and other businesses that provide goods and services.
- *Office buildings:* Spaces where managerial, operational and clerical activities, administrative duties and employee meetings are performed.
- *Industrial buildings:* Structures utilised for manufacturing and production operations. Examples include factories, distribution warehouses and data centres.

The pros of commercial property investing

Let's begin with the upside. Here are some of the significant advantages of investing in commercial property.

Triple net leases

A 'triple net lease' is an arrangement in which the tenant is responsible for covering all the outgoing expenses: property taxes, property insurance, maintenance costs. There are watered-down versions in the form of double net and single net leases, which require less of the tenant.

With a residential lease, while a tenant is often on the hook for their water and electricity usage and insuring their possessions, the landlord pays to have everything connected and the building insured.

Of course, a triple net lease is not guaranteed in every contract, so you'll want a good commercial lawyer to represent you and negotiate the best terms and conditions.

Flexibility

There are certain terms in a residential lease that are just non-negotiable. Renters have rights and protections that are written into residential tenancy laws in each state. In a commercial lease, there is much more wiggle room. You can negotiate a great many things that you simply couldn't in a residential tenancy agreement. For instance, you might negotiate into the deal that at the end of the tenancy, the occupant must repaint, recarpet and restore the space into the condition it was in prior to occupancy. Just imagine asking that of your residential renter. Good luck.

Another aspect of flexibility involves the operating hours of businesses. Most have *off hours* in which you would be able to gain access if, for example, the air conditioning failed and you needed to have it fixed. That could be done after hours without disrupting operations.

Less turnover

One of the key selling points of a commercial property investment is the fact that businesses tend to stay in place for a while. As much of a hassle as it is to move yourself from one house to another, it's much, much more difficult to move a business, which generally requires an expensive fit-out to suit the nature of the business. If it's a restaurant, for instance, that means installing all the kitchen equipment, creating ample space for a dining room, and maybe a lot of extra bathroom fixtures if it's a heavily frequented establishment.

Every business has its own needs, and fitting out a space is an expensive proposition. It's something you don't want to do frequently. So, when a business moves in, they are going to want to stay long enough to make it worth their while. That usually means a multi-year lease with an opportunity for them to renew it for another couple of multi-year terms.

The lessee is going to want the security that comes with knowing they're not going to have to up and move after a short amount of time. And as a landlord, that means peace of mind that the building will be occupied for a lengthy period and won't be sitting vacant any time soon.

Businesses also need to stay in one place because that's where their customers know to find them. For some types of business, it's important to establish a presence in the community, or to appear to be set to stay a long time, as opposed to being seen as a fly-by-night. Most businesses choose a location because that's where their key demographic lives or works.

~

These factors make being a commercial landlord attractive. But then again, it can get quite difficult if that business does decide to leave. And that leads us to …

The cons of commercial property investing

Despite the promise of excellent returns, investing in commercial properties also comes with risks. Depending on the economic environment and level of competition, a commercial property could be empty for several months between tenancies. You also need to make a more considerable initial investment to purchase a commercial property, especially if it's in a desirable location. In addition, lenders often require a larger minimum deposit.

Let's begin with the problem of what happens when your business tenant *does* leave.

Vacancies

So, your tenant moves out. Now you're sitting on an expensive piece of property that's empty and stripped bare. Getting someone else to take on a new lease often requires a rent-free period, which could be as short as a month or as long as even six months. That provides the business an opportunity to re-fit the space to their particular requirements.

Even if your tenant seems committed to stick around for the long haul, there could be circumstances beyond their control which affect their ability to fulfill the lease. Suppose you own a lucrative property in an upscale mall. But one day, the bank moves out of the mall – they're doing that more and more in Australia and around the world as they are getting rid of their brick-and-mortar stores in exchange for a digital business online.

A bank is an anchor. If an anchor falls, you're on a sinking ship. The anchor brings in business that adjacent businesses cash in on. A consumer may drive 10 minutes to visit their bank or to shop at a large department store, but wouldn't do the same to grab a coffee. But the coffee shop next door to their bank or the store where everyone wants to shop is going to get that business simply by virtue of its proximity and convenience.

The idea here is that, just like with the stock market, there are variables that are outside of your control. There are even variables that are outside the control of your tenant that will nonetheless determine the course of their business.

Ask yourself if the slightly higher rental return of a commercial property is worth the risk of long vacancy periods … and the resultant handouts to lure a new business to your property.

Complexity

The contract required for a commercial lease is not the standard 12-month tenancy agreement you would sign for a residential property. That's boilerplate stuff that you can do on your own. But here, you are actually engaging in a commercial contract. As such, you need to involve solicitors to draft commercial lease agreements. And that is an additional cost. And recall, being able to negotiate the lease was listed earlier as a *pro*, in that it provides flexibility. But realise that flexibility comes at a cost.

Lack of comparable properties

Another drawback of investing in commercial property is the lack of comparable properties on the market. Residential real estate establishes values very easily, and there's rarely much gap between the appraisals of buyer and seller. There are enough similar properties being bought and sold, and frequently enough, to clearly set a floor and ceiling on any property's value.

Not so with a commercial property. Each is unique. There is a lot of data to include in the equation when it comes to valuing a non-residential property. You can't simply look at recent sales in the area. It doesn't matter if it's a similar-sized building or parcel of land, or even whether it's the lot right next door. One might have better parking access or greater visibility or better foot traffic. These are variables that significantly alter the valuation.

Each transaction reinvents the wheel; no two are exactly alike. You're not comparing apples to apples. And that means there is a lot more negotiation involved in determining the appropriate value of any property.

Lending limitations

Making matters even more difficult for the investor is that lenders look much more favourably on residential loans than commercial loans. That goes back to the fact that everyone needs somewhere to live – it's fundamental. Lenders understand that businesses fail more often than do people, and with less consequence. Giving money to a business is a bigger role of the dice.

Zoning

When you buy a commercial property, that piece of land is permitted for certain kinds of businesses but not others. You might be able to brew coffee, but not drill for oil. You might be zoned to operate an office with a limited number of people, but might not be able to open a hair salon. There are bylaws that need to be identified and understood before making any serious long-term decisions with any commercial piece of property. And that introduces the expenses associated with conducting solid due diligence.

Chapter 6

The 'rentvesting' strategy

Quite often, people simply can't afford to buy the home they see themselves living in. Maybe that's because they prefer to live near the beach, or they want a couple of extra bedrooms and a big backyard, or maybe there's a certain school catchment area they would like to have their children in – or any number of other reasons that prevent them from owning the home in which they want to reside. But that doesn't mean they are excluded from the real estate market. On the contrary, it is in fact important that they get onto the real estate ladder sooner rather than later, so that one day they *will* be able to buy the home of their dreams.

What is Rentvesting?

Rentvesting is an investment strategy that involves renting a property to live in that's right for your lifestyle, while you purchase an investment property in a suburb that is more affordable.

The Seven Key Advantages of Rentvesting

I have identified seven Key Advantages of Rentvesting. Here they are in no particular order.

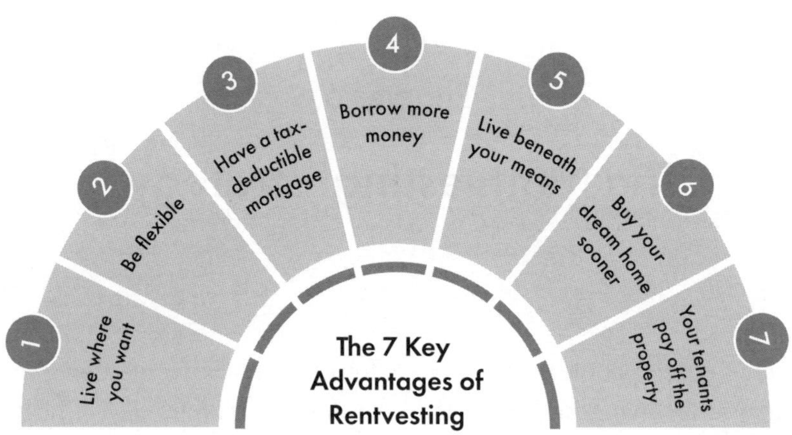

Advantage 1: Live where you want

Rentvesting allows you to get into the market and start building a property portfolio without actually living in your own property. While renting a home, you can then buy wherever the property clock says it's the ideal time to buy. (See chapter 7 for an explanation of the property clock.) Maybe you are living in Victoria, but there's a booming community in Perth where some massive infrastructure projects are being developed. Well, you don't want to pull the kids out of school, leave your job, and move off to Perth. But that doesn't mean you can't buy property there and keep living where you currently are.

Maybe you just want to live in the city or near the beach, but you can't afford to buy there. Capital growth in desirable postcodes significantly outpaces rental growth, which is anchored by inflationary patterns. The lifestyle opportunities in these locations are particularly attractive to young people, and there is generally a greater range of employment opportunities located there.

An appealing apartment in the city might run you $600 a week in rent, but as much as $900 a week if you were having to service a mortgage on that same property.

Advantage 2: Be flexible

A lot of younger people rentvest to get ahead. It provides them an opportunity to build a property portfolio around the country while living close to the place they work. Their employment may require them to relocate as they take promotions or if they change jobs. Given that they are most likely only on a year-to-year lease, a rentvestor can easily pick up and move into another rental property, far less tethered to the property they're leaving behind.

Their employment is what's making possible their property buying in the beginning, until their portfolio begins generating enough revenue that they are no longer chained to that particular job. When they start earning enough in investment profits, they have a lot more decision-making power about where they want to live and how they want to make money – whether passively *and* actively, or entirely passively.

For many, rentvesting is a best-of-both-worlds scenario. You get to live where you want to, while still enjoying the capital growth of property ownership. It can allow for great flexibility. I speak from experience. When I bought my first house, I moved right in and it became my primary residence. But not long afterward – within 12 months – my job moved me to far-off Singapore.

It was while I was living in Singapore that I spent a great deal of time researching and educating myself about the key drivers of real estate investing. So, when I moved back, rather than returning to the house I had purchased and had been living in, I moved to

Sydney, where my job had landed me. I made the decision to rent out my house and become a rentvestor while living in a beautiful apartment overlooking the ocean.

I made a judgment call, deciding I could grow wealth faster by leveraging real estate, buying multiple houses, while renting at the same time. It was the best decision I ever made. Rather than selling my first house and simply buying a new, more expensive house in blue-chip Sydney, and getting stuck with a massive mortgage – which would have stopped me right in my tracks – I used the capital growth I had acquired to leverage into more houses in better-positioned markets.

Advantage 3: Have a tax-deductible mortgage

Unlike homebuyers, who end up with substantial non-tax-deductible debt, as a rentvestor, you can claim the interest on all of your mortgage repayments associated with your investment property every fiscal year. That can not only boost your cashflow, but also help to reduce your personal income tax liability.

It gets better. You can also claim various expenses associated with the management and upkeep of your property. You may additionally be able to claim depreciation, making property ownership a lot more affordable.

Advantage 4: Borrow more money

Your income from the rent you charge will go towards servicing your debt. So, you can essentially borrow more for an investment property than you could for your main residence, depending on a few variables like the lender's terms and conditions. As your equity goes up, you can draw on that equity to use as the deposit on your second property.

Then, the rent from both properties goes towards servicing that debt. And each time the capital value goes up, you can refinance to use more equity to borrow money to grow your wealth using leverage.

You're now on a faster track to getting your next property.

Advantage 5: Live beneath your means

There's no rule that says your residence needs to be your biggest investment. In fact, by living beneath your means, you can save more quickly for your next property purchase.

This may be particularly important for younger investors who might be more content in a smaller place or one that does not require much upkeep on their part. If you are living in your first property, you will have some expenses that a renter wouldn't. You will likely also have to commit more of your time to maintaining that property.

Advantage 6: Buy your dream home sooner (and with less debt)

By focusing solely on property as an investment, you will be better positioned to research the market before entering it as an informed homebuyer with equity built from your existing investment portfolio. The capital growth and market knowledge you gain while waiting to buy your own home will help you secure the right one quicker, with less debt and less stress than most first-time homebuyers.

Advantage 7: Your tenants pay off the property

While you are happily renting the place where you prefer to live, your tenants will be busy paying off your mortgage.

Ideally, you want to hold a positively or neutrally geared property in which the rental income covers the costs associated with servicing your loan and the other expenses that are part and parcel of owning the property.

This cashflow strategy is relatively easy to achieve in a low-interest-rate environment. Over time, you will be able to increase the rent you charge, and as a result the property will become positively geared, meaning that your asset is making you money.

Interest rates decisions are made by the Reserve Bank of Australia's (RBA) Board. The official interest rate is also referred to as the cash rate. In Australia, interest rates averaged 3.87% from 1990 until 2022, reaching an all-time high of 17.50% in January 1990 and a record low of 0.10 percent in November 2020 due to the global pandemic.

It would be safe to expect that the RBA will continue adjusting the cash rate until it reaches a more stable range of 2% to 3%.

~

As you can see, there are a lot of good reasons to consider rent-vesting as a viable option. Whether it is the best strategy for you depends on your goals, your circumstances and your desires when it comes to where you want to live.

Chapter 7

The 5-Pillar Property Growth Model for identifying the best locations

When you're choosing your primary residence, you are probably evaluating what we might call 'lifestyle' features. You want a place that strikes you on an emotional level. It would have to be close to your work, near the locations you prefer to frequent – say, the beach or an upscale shopping centre – maybe within a good school catchment area, or perhaps just close to where your friends or family live.

In other words, you are probably not taking into account the key drivers of capital growth, or looking at data to determine demographic shifts, or researching other dry statistical information. But this type of numbers-based information happens to be exactly what you should be drawing on when making an *investment* decision.

I represent both types of clients: homebuyers *and* investors. My homebuyers are obviously driven by the emotional reasons above. But, so are many of my investors … at least, initially. I often need to educate new investors on a completely different approach that requires a totally new mindset. And that's how, over the past 20 or so years of buying real estate all across Australia, I developed this reliable 5-Pillar Property Growth Model.

All five pillars must be strong and in alignment to ensure you have indeed found the ideal location. The more success you have with each individual pillar, the better your chance of making more capital growth in a shorter period, which will allow you to get back into the market sooner for your next investment. Of course, getting each pillar right requires a lot of data-driven research along with a rational rather than emotional state of mind. Remember, it's a numbers game.

The 5-Pillar Property Growth Model

I will list the pillars here and then go into each in detail:

1. The property cycle
2. Key statistics
3. Local infrastructure
4. Demographics
5. Cashflow.

The 5-Pillar Property Growth Model for identifying the best locations

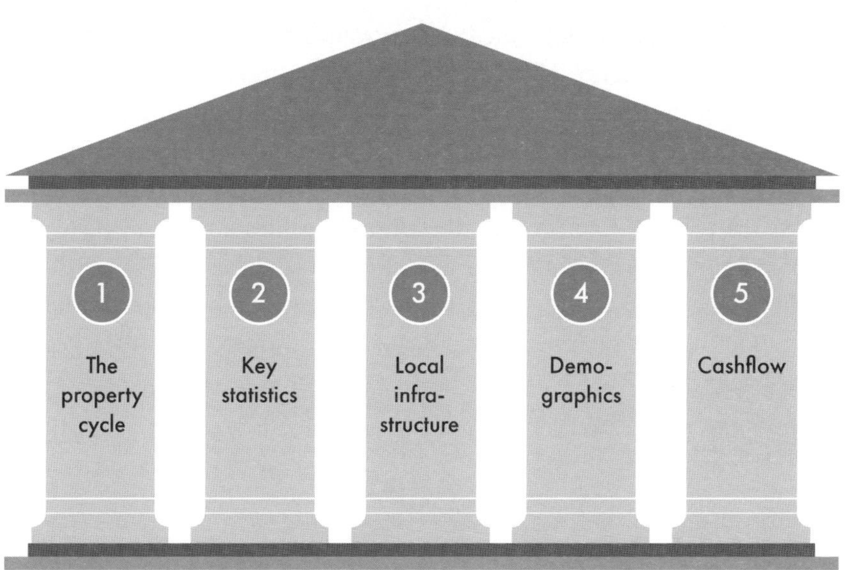

Pillar 1: The property cycle

The property cycle in any country around the globe should be looked at the same. Basically, real estate goes through repeating cycles from boom to downturn to bottoming out to recovery to growth to boom again, when it will plateau before eventually and inevitably turning south and repeating the cycle in perpetuity.

The property clock

The property clock uses the face of a clock (obviously) to represent the phase the market is currently in. It might be at 12, peaking. Or headed toward 2 or 3 and waning. Or down at 6, bottoming out. Or on the upswing, rising again among the larger numbers.

It is imperative you know where you are in the cycle. Fortunately, there is enough data out there that you can identify the phase you're in. I find the clock produced by Herron Todd White to be reliable and independent.* They value properties on behalf of mortgage providers – when someone goes for a home loan or some other type of investment loan, the bank will request an appraisal on the value of the property. This company is one of the largest independent property valuation firms in Australia and they process many valuations around the country each month. They have a huge amount of information going into their database. So when the numbers are crunched there is a vast number of datapoints, which provides a clear picture of where any given property is situated on the cycle.

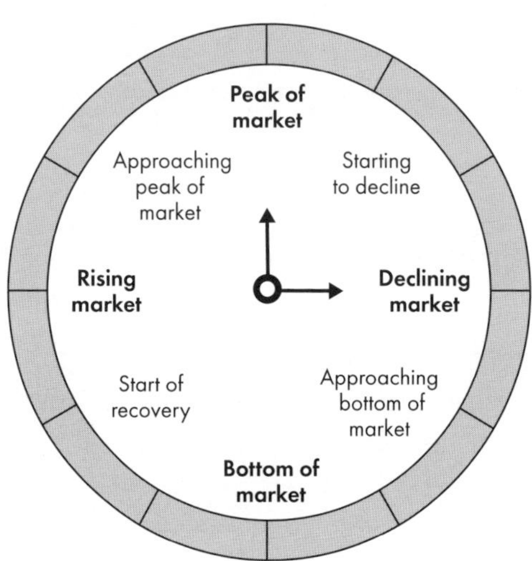

And here's another fortunate thing: the property cycle is unique in each state and territory of Australia. And that's important for an

* Go to: www.htw.com.au/month-in-review.

investor because it means it's always a good time to buy *somewhere*. You just need to know where.

In addition, the cycle is different depending on the *type* of property. Commercial or rural properties may be overpriced while residential properties are simultaneously undervalued. Or vice versa. But then, the opposite may be true in a neighbouring state.

Drill down further and you may find that freestanding houses are in one phase of the cycle, while apartments are in a wholly different phase. And then, within each state, there are various regions that also operate independently, meaning that there is a lot of data that needs processing to locate the best investment possibilities.

The property cycle becomes much more complex the deeper you delve into it. But understanding the cycle can indicate what times and regions are currently favourable for investing.

I've talked to investors who have told me, 'I bought a property seven years ago, but it hasn't made any money.' And you have to wonder about that … until you find out they bought at the peak of the cycle.

Historically, property has tended to double in value every seven to 12 years. Over time, the data bears that out. As I write, Sydney's property market is running quite hot. It's artificially overpriced. Wages haven't kept up with property prices, which went up when the cash rate was lowered. As the cash rate declines, the average family can borrow more. Their serviceability therefore goes up because they have more access to low-interest money.

Those investors who bought at peak market value will just have to wait until the market corrects itself. It will take moving into a new growth cycle for that piece of property to begin paying off.

That kind of mistake could have been prevented by simply identifying which phase of the cycle the market was in at the time of purchase. The ideal time to buy is in a recovery phase. Yes, you are bound to make an ultimately larger return if you invest at the bottom of the cycle. But that is going to take significantly longer to peak. Buying in the recovery phase ensures the most capital growth in the shortest period of time.

Property cycles are predictable to a certain degree. And there are a number of factors that can influence their phases. A financial crisis, for example, can devastate a market. Then again, it could cause home values to skyrocket. That's one of the problems with such factors: it may be clear that they will impact the market, but it isn't necessarily clear *how*.

Pillar 2: Key statistics

I'm a numbers guy. I love what most people would consider dull, boring charts, graphs, statistics and other data-driven information. As they say, *numbers don't lie*.

Vacancy rental rate

One key statistic I start with is the *vacancy rental rate*. How many properties are empty as a percentage in a particular suburb?

What is a healthy vacancy rate? In Australia, 3% is considered a healthy vacancy rate. That figure means there is a good ratio of available properties. Tenants can be a bit choosy and investors can get their properties rented rather quickly. It's a balanced equation for both sides.

There are locations at 1% vacancy. That's good for investors, at least at first glance. Scarcity drives up prices. But for would-be tenants, it means turning up for an open house and there's 50, 60, 70 people fighting to outbid each other. On the flipside, if there's a greater degree of vacancy, that means renters have greater bargaining power and can wait longer to make decisions.

But ultimately, an investor should be looking to own a property in an area with a low to healthy vacancy rate. Why? Because you don't want a high degree of tenant turnover and you don't want a rental property to sit vacant. If your tenant feels like they have overpaid, they're going to leave for a fairer-priced place when they get the chance.

Historical capital growth

Another important statistic I look closely at is *historical capital growth*. While history does not predict what will happen in the future, if you have enough datapoints you can begin to see trends and trajectories, and get a clearer image of where things are heading.

If you see capital growth dwindling over time, you probably don't want to be gambling on a sudden and miraculous turnaround. You probably want to wait until you see an upswing and feel a bit more certain that the tide is rising.

You can often buy a property at a cheap price, but you need to know whether it is still going to lose another 10% of its value before it begins to flatten off. If it hasn't hit rock bottom, you don't want to buy in yet. There is no sense in losing money in the short term simply because it's undervalued and will eventually begin turning a profit.

Average days on market

Another factor I find very important is *average days on market*. The longer the days required to sell, the greater the buyer's negotiating power. Of course, if the average days on market is on the high side, you need to ask yourself why. Is there something wrong with the area you weren't aware of? Is the property overpriced? Why is it taking so long to sell?

When the average number is on the short side, and at the time of writing it's as low as a few days in some markets, that's a different kind of problem, but a problem nonetheless. Buyers will bid sight-unseen, forgoing the due diligence that is so important in analysing a property. A market environment such as this is dangerous ground for a cautious investor.

Number of properties sold per quarter

Another key statistic to bear in mind is the number of properties sold per quarter. If you begin to plot the number of properties being sold each quarter, you can begin to determine if sales are picking up, are stagnant or are dropping. It's a barometer to measure demand. If you find, for instance, that the number of properties being sold is on a steady incline over the past several quarters, you can fairly surmise that there are many more would-be buyers who have not yet got in but who are looking for their opportunity. In other words, there is likely a demand that will fuel a resultant surge in prices.

Pillar 3: Demographics

A statistical category that is so all-encompassing and overarching that it deserves its own pillar is the wealth of data that falls under the umbrella of *demographics*. Population-related information is more than just interesting or informative, it can also be reliably predictive.

This may sound almost self-evident, but it's worth stating because often the most simplistic of ideas – because they go without saying – also seem to go without considering: you want to buy in an area where people want to go. I know, the clouds are parting and you're having a revelation. But let's really break down what that means, and more importantly, what that looks like in real-world terms.

Population growth (or decline)

Governments and businesses spend a great deal of resources forecasting population growth. Why do they do that? It's because they want to be able to serve growing communities, albeit for different reasons. Governments do so because that's what they are elected to do – to serve people. Businesses have a more profit-driven, but no less important, motive. When they see a growing community, they see an untapped market they want to be the first to enter.

In America, they have a mythical figure called 'Johnny Appleseed'. He is depicted as a happy-go-lucky barefoot wanderer planting apple seeds for the sheer joy of it. The truth, however, is that the early United States had a policy that required new settlements to have an existing apple orchard. Apples were not consumed so much as fruit, but were the primary ingredient in a hard liquor known as 'applejack'. Strong drink played an important role in frontier society, and as such, it was determined that a local source was necessary before building a new town.

Johnny Appleseed was not so much an eccentric drifter as a speculative real estate developer. Jonathan Chapman – his real name – scouted the most logical new settlement locations along the frontiers of Pennsylvania, Ohio, Indiana, Illinois and other then-uncharted territories, searching far afield for prime plots of land where the future groups of Westbound homesteaders would eventually settle, and then buying them.

He understood that frontier communities soon outgrew their boundaries and the children of settlers continued moving farther West. And he knew what they were looking for: a source of fresh water, plenty of game, arable soil and so forth. More importantly, he knew they also needed an apple orchard. And so he planted them years in advance, then nurtured them to maturity, so that when the frontier finally caught up, the settlers wouldn't have to think twice about buying up his plots of land. Those orchards were in a sense the first appearance of a prefab real estate development. The apple orchards drew in residents. (Later in this chapter, we'll see how hospitals, universities, shopping centres and other large public- and private-sector infrastructure projects also behave like magnets, attracting new residents.)

With regard to demographics, there are two ways in which communities grow:

- The first is over time, by reproduction. Looking at birth rates, you can determine long-term trends. It can be encouraging if families continue to have children at a higher rate. If they stopped having kids year after year, that would be cause for concern.
- The second is, in the shorter term, communities grow or shrink as people move in or move out. Internal net migration is a measure of the number of people moving into one state from another. That's a meaningful piece of information. It can tell you what spots are hot. At the time of writing, tens of thousands of people are migrating to Queensland from New South Wales and Victoria. Whether it's to live on a larger piece of property, to experience a richer lifestyle, or enjoy a better work/life balance, they've made the determination that moving out of state is the best way to accomplish that goal.

By studying demographic data, you can figure out if a location is growing or dying, and if it's the result of people staying and having children or out-of-staters coming and going. That information is not mere trivia. It tells a story if you are able to fill in the details with other critical data, and if you're willing to listen.

Who lives in the area?

Knowing *who* lives in a given community will provide you some clues about where that community is headed from an investment standpoint. What do those residents do for work? Do they have blue-collar jobs at a local factory or warehouse, for example? Let's say that's the case. So, what is the future of that particular industry? Maybe it's a fossil fuel refinery or coal mine, and the region is rapidly moving towards wind or solar power. What do you think is going to happen with all those employees in this community who may be out of work before long? As you can tell, demographics and infrastructure are interwoven and influence each other in impactful ways.

As you look at properties, remember you want to find one that is symbolic of the surrounding neighbourhood. So, it's important to know who is buying in the area. Are they families with two kids and a dog? Are they busy professional couples? Are they retired folks? What's the average age? It doesn't make a lot of sense to buy a five- or six-bedroom house if almost everyone on the block is under 30 years old and without children. Neither would you want to buy a two-storey house on a street where everyone is elderly and may have trouble with stairs.

It's also helpful to know what type of income people are bringing in. You don't want to financially distress your tenants. If you're stretching their budget too thin, you won't be able to raise the rent because they won't be able to pay it. And if your property is a constantly revolving door, with tenants moving in and out because they can't afford the annual uptick in rent, you've made an investment mistake.

As a general rule of thumb, you don't want your tenant spending more than about 30% of their income to service the rent. They obviously have other expenses, some of which are luxuries, so if the rent goes up, they can easily adjust their excesses to meet the financial obligation. That's why I prefer to invest in a slightly higher household income area than a slightly lower one. The better off your tenants are, financially speaking, the easier it will be for them to handle regular rental increases.

Owner-occupied vs rented properties

Next, you want to consider the ratio of owner-occupied properties to rented properties in an area. You don't want potential renters to have an overwhelming amount of choice when your rental goes on the market. If there are a lot of options, you will probably have to lower your asking price to be competitive and fill your vacancy quickly. A little bit of scarcity ensures you can ask more in rent.

Another reason this statistic is important is, by and large, owner-occupied properties are better maintained. A house-proud neighbourhood is good for home values. House-proud homeowners cut their lawns like golf greens, they keep a fresh coat of paint on their fences, they grow roses, they 'keep up with the Joneses'.

In a neighbourhood that is predominantly rentals, residents often don't feel the embarrassment or stigma of failing to maintain the property. They don't *own* the place, after all, and so they aren't as invested. They also may not plan to live there for a long time, so they may not feel a great deal of obligation to their neighbours. And they may have chosen to rent simply to avoid the regular chores associated with home ownership.

However, when you find a neighbourhood that has predominantly house-proud owners with a few rentals scattered in between, you find that those renters tend to keep up their yards and their homes to match everyone else on the street. People usually try to fit in wherever they are.

This phenomenon happens in the opposite direction, too, though. If it's not a house-proud neighbourhood, and a person sees their neighbour's lawn hasn't been cut in a few weeks, that person is more likely to let it go as well. The neighbourhood begins to take on the sloppiness of those who neglect upkeep.

This is the 'broken windows' theory, which essentially states that where there's a building with a broken window, people feel that nobody there really cares about the neighbourhood. As a result, other examples of disrepair or vandalism – rampant weeds, empty beer cans, shattered glass, trash, graffiti, maybe even gangs – begin to crop up. When they do, it's very difficult to undo the damage and restore the quality of the neighbourhood. That's why it's so important to fix that first broken window right away.

And again, the owner-to-renter ratio will provide a pretty accurate forecast for the physical appearance of the neighbourhood. It should also ensure that vacancies will be less frequent and that you'll have a better overall experience.

Pillar 4: Local infrastructure

When I look at a particular area to buy in, I want to know what's happening in that area. What's going to drive growth? What's going to attract new residents? The answer, as it is so often, is *money*. That is to say, if there is public and/or private financing of new or existing large-scale projects, it will create a ripple effect throughout the area. If tens or hundreds of millions of dollars, or billions of dollars, are being committed to a new development, it will necessarily impact everything in the vicinity.

The bellwethers of growth

Think about the effect of constructing a new hospital, university, shopping centre or amusement park. Whether it's government or private industry, or any combination of the two, you can rest assured they have spared no expense in identifying the right location to invest their resources. Mistakes are just so very costly. They have consulted experts, studied the data and done their due diligence to find the ideal place to develop their project.

Consider everything involved in a massive construction project. To begin with, a whole lot of people have to be employed in the design and construction. From architects to steelworkers to carpenters to plumbers to interior designers, there are a lot of jobs created just to build and fill out the physical structure. And all those people will need servicing. They will eat lunch nearby, go out for beers after work, maybe put their children in the local school, maybe even rent a home with a relatively short commute to the site.

And when the thing is built, it will obviously be filled with employees. Let's say it's a university. Well, of course you have the administrative staff and all the professors. But you will also have the caretakers, the groundskeepers, the cafeteria workers, the campus security guards and myriad other jobs that will need to be filled.

With all the new jobs at the university, they'll probably need to widen the highway to make room for all the new commuters. They may want to add a train line, too. Guess what? That's even more jobs. Well, with all these new people now employed in the area – not to mention all the students who will be attending this campus – the town is probably going to need more restaurants to feed them. It will need more grocery markets, office supply stores, clothing stores, a movie theatre – even a big, fancy entertainment district. And then, maybe even a car dealership and a bicycle shop to get people around. More jobs!

Of course, with all these people and all this new construction, the local government may realise that there are going to be some accidents. People are going to get hurt on the job or in a crash on the way to work. Or they may just decide that with their newfound stability, it's time to have a child. So, now it's time to build a new hospital. And everything I just described continues on, expanding on itself.

What happens to the property in the area? Suddenly, this is a very lucrative and desirable place to own a home. People want to live near the university, the restaurant district or their job, let's say, at the new hospital. The homes that are adjacent to, within or that surround this new commercial hub will benefit greatly from their presence and rise in value accordingly.

Now, if you knew in advance that the university was going to be built, and you invested in a house that would adequately suit the professor and his or her family, or the medical worker and their family who want to live close to work, you would probably be turning a nice, tidy profit, wouldn't you?

Major infrastructure projects significantly impact an area's property clock. Sites are chosen because they appear to be ready to enjoy an upswing. The clock ticks. Announcements are made about the project and investors take notice, realising there will be opportunities. Tick. Construction begins. Tick. And, as discussed above, a variety of other businesses announce plans to locate in the area and then begin construction … then, a train stop, a luxury hotel, a new development of homes. Every new improvement influences the clock, as it ticks steadily up towards 12.

Everywhere I go, I talk to sales agents, property managers, building inspectors – everyone on the ground who might be privy to the latest information. The idea is to find a diamond in the rough. When you see a neighbourhood that is on the inexpensive side and you start seeing some well-known multinational businesses come in – an Ikea, a McDonald's, a Costco – you know these companies have done their due diligence and spent a lot of time and money to determine where to place their next location. They are putting their money where their mouth is.

For an investor, when you are seeing such businesses move in, it provides you a pretty solid, reliable forecast. And getting early word of anticipated growth is, I can almost guarantee you, better than any stock tip you're likely to get on the golf course.

Pillar 5: Cashflow

The last of my five pillars is cashflow. People always seem to overlook this very important item. Frankly, I find it mind blowing. Remember why you got into this: to *make money*. Real estate investing needs to be approached like a business, not a hobby.

When you are considering purchasing an investment property, begin by forecasting your income. Once you establish a weekly income rate, estimate all the related expenses: what are the council rates, the water rates, the insurances, the property management fees? What will maintenance cost you? Factor those in. And don't forget to add in the interest payments on your loan. If the property appreciates or depreciates in value, be prepared for that as well.

I often talk to potential investors who are looking to be negatively geared for tax purposes, and they want to write some of that off. I have to remind them, 'Look, if you're paying tax on the thing, it generally means that you're making money from it, which is kind of the whole point.' I explain that they are confusing investments with tax strategies. Negative gearing only provides short-term cashflow, which can be great. But you don't make big decisions based on tax-minimising strategies. You don't buy a property with the idea of losing money on it. That's not a good plan.

Where does this idea come from? A lot of places, actually. Someone will read something on social media, or they'll find a glossy advert in the paper. The gist is usually the same: 'We'll save you tax – buy a property.' Sounds great, right? But when you reverse-engineer what they're saying, it's basically, the property is going to cost you a whole lot of money and run at a loss and – here's the silver lining – *you can claim that loss against your income*.

Why would you invest in something – anything – that promises you going in that you are about to lose money? I mean, if you want to approach things that way, you could just give me $50,000, I could go out back and burn it for you, and call it a win–win. Hey, you can claim that as a loss and count it against your income!

It's just faulty logic.

Investors need to forecast all the potential costs associated with holding their property and then make sure they can cover the shortfall; negative gearing will allow investors to recover some of the expenses in tax savings. Nonetheless, you need to be confident that your property will deliver long-term capital growth so that these losses will be ultimately offset by large profits into the future.

There is nothing wrong with a negatively geared property and this approach can be a tax-effective strategy for a period of time, but always with the strategy that the property will soon become neutrally, then positively geared once the rental income increases over time. In the long run, you won't mind the taxes because that's evidence you're making a nice profit.

~

In conclusion, the market will go up as the population grows, which increases demand. When infrastructure goes in, people spend money, which drives wages in the area. When vacancies get tight, the scarcity drives up the price of rents. It's a perfect storm for the recovery phase on the property clock. The five pillars are applicable to the property cycles, and when all five are aligned, you know that a particular area is primed for growth.

If you get each of those five pillars right, you will be making highly informed decisions and, as a result, you're going to have much more success. This is a scientific approach that I have spent many years developing. If you follow it, you're going to have a much better experience than if you take your chances on some other, less analytical method.

I spoke to a woman recently who told me about a painful experience she had with an apartment she bought. She had not followed my strategy, and it was a missed opportunity as she basically set herself back five years that could have been spent getting into her next property. At the very least, she could have spared herself the countless headaches she described having as a result. She told me, 'I'm never going to buy property again … without talking to you first.'

But even if you *have* made a mistake, don't beat yourself up over it. It's over and done. I advise people in such situations to look forward, not backward. There's no point dwelling on the past; the point is, you've made a decision now to do it differently next time. Enjoy that because that's ultimately what matters.

Chapter 8

The 7 Deadly Sins of Property Investment

After so many years in this industry, having bought hundreds of properties and talked with thousands of people about real estate, I have learned a lot about what works… and what *doesn't*.

I like to start a conversation with questions about a person's goals, aspirations and experience with property investing. I like to find out what they would like to improve upon. And wow, have I heard a lot of horror stories in my time. These candid discussions about common mistakes have become the basis for what I refer to as The 7 Deadly Sins of Property Investment.

I always advise the people with whom I speak that they can call me whenever they need if they have a question. If I can help someone avoid a potentially disastrous buying decision or offer a bit of wisdom or guidance, it might save that person years of financial hardship, remorse or perhaps conflict with their partner. I might be able to help them avoid one of The 7 Deadly Sins of Property Investment.

The 7 Deadly Sins

So, here they are:

1. Buying close to home
2. Becoming emotional
3. Worrying about tax
4. Ignoring the property cycle
5. Buying the wrong type of property
6. Flipping
7. Managing the property yourself

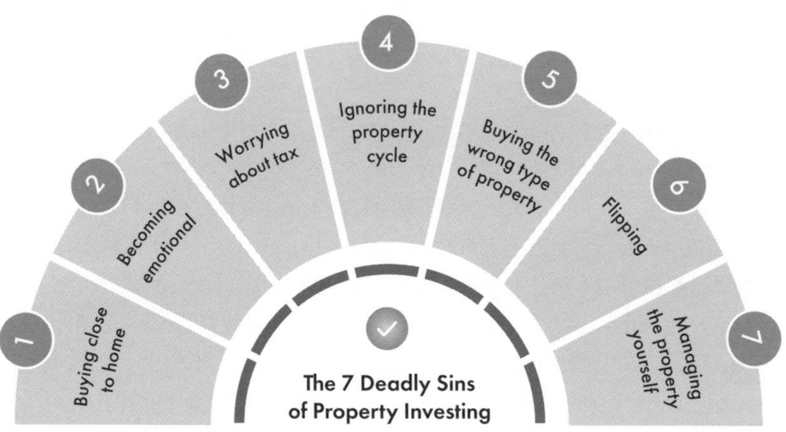

Let's look at each of these more closely.

Sin 1: Buying close to home

The number-one mistake I find when someone is considering buying an investment property is that they are making their decision based on how *close* the location is to where they live. There's nothing wrong *per se* about buying an investment property nearby, but if that is your primary factor in choosing the property, that is definitely a recipe for disaster.

There are several reasons people give me for basing their decision on proximity. Often, it is a matter of convenience. They know the area, they want something nearby. Think about where you tend to get free advice – at a barbecue, a dinner party, the golf course, wherever you are chatting with your friends or family, or other locals. But you are not getting independent, objective – or expert – information. There is an inherent bias that people who are not industry professionals have for their own community or region.

I can't tell you how many times I've heard someone say they want to buy locally because if something goes wrong, they can quickly go over there and fix the broken *fill-in-the-blank*, whatever it might be. Of course, this is a terrible idea. You should never be intruding on your tenants. You hire a property manager to act as your liaison. It is that person's job to hire the right licensed and insured professional to handle any maintenance issues that arise.

I have had conversations with property investors who have explained that they had not raised the rent on their tenants even after several years. Why not? *Guilt.* They go over there and they talk to and get to know the people living there, and then they don't feel quite right about mandating an annual rent increase.

I bought a house not long ago that was tenanted. They had been living there for six years. And in all that time, there had not been an increase in the rent. It was a lovely house, well located, nicely maintained. It was being under-rented by as much as $125 a week. When I purchased it, I found out why. The landlord had been looking after it himself, and had of course met the tenant and built up a relationship.

If you are a generous person and want to provide for other people's rent, that is certainly your prerogative, but that isn't really what *investing* is. Again, this is a business; the idea is to make the most money in the shortest amount of time. That requires looking further afield and making sure you are buying in the right location. If you want to buy something close to your home, be certain that it is driven by facts and figures, and that it aligns with each of the five pillars.

Sin 2: Becoming emotional

The next most prevalent issue I encounter is that a person becomes wrapped up emotionally in the buying decision. As much as property is capable of resonating with us on a instinctual level, at the end of the day investing is more science than art. It really doesn't matter what *you* think of a property, what ultimately matters is what your target demographic thinks of it. Don't picture yourself living there. In fact, simply remove yourself from the equation and be objective.

You don't like the colour of the splashback tiles above the sink? Who cares? You are not the one who has to look at it every day, are you? And furthermore, has anyone really ever walked away from a home they were considering because of splashback tiles? Is that a dealbreaker for anyone? I'm pretty sure you have never heard someone say, 'It was truly our dream home, but then we saw those purple splashback tiles, and well … '

I've also heard that a certain property was 'too far from the golf course'. Well, not everyone golfs, do they? Maybe it's close to shopping centres or to the beach. Most folks enjoy the beach. And again, that's who you are buying for: *most folks*. What is the largest demographic in the area looking for in a home? Whatever that is, you want to be investing in it.

It's also important that you remain detached during the negotiation phase. You have to be willing to walk away. I have come across properties where the seller is only selling because they are financially distressed, which is terrible. It is not something I ever like to see. But then, you've got buyers who are saying, 'Oh, let's give them some more money,' because they feel a sense of compassion for the person. I know of some really good charities, and I am more than happy to recommend them, but that is an entirely separate transaction to a house purchase.

If you want to invest in property, invest in property. If you want to give money to people in need, by all means, please do so. But you should not confuse the two, as they are separate spheres and require entirely different analyses.

Sin 3: Worrying about tax

As I've explained, property investing is a long-term strategy to make money, not a short-term way to trim your tax bill. You don't buy an asset with the intention of losing money unless you are running a money-laundering scheme, in which case you will probably soon have larger problems than finding the ideal investment strategy.

Nevertheless, I hear this line of thinking repeated again and again. Generally, someone just came across an advert that sounded like a good idea at the time. Tax minimisation should be considered incidental to your investment plan, not the basis of it.

Sin 4: Ignoring the property cycle

It's always the right time to buy *somewhere*. The flipside of that, however, is that it's always the wrong time to buy somewhere else. There is no genius in knowing *when* to buy, the brilliance is knowing *where* to buy – and getting that right is the result of extensive research and data analysis.

The property cycle is unique to every city and suburb in every state. Some tides are rising while others are ebbing. The key to successful growth is finding properties that are at the recovery point or in a rising market phase.

This is just one reason, obviously, that buying a property simply because it happens to be close to home is a bad strategy. If there is another location in a better market phase, why would you not buy *there*? Of course, if you are buying the home that you plan to live in, and it's a declining market phase but you absolutely want to live there, that is not so much an investment decision as it is a choice about where you want to reside.

Sin 5: Buying the wrong type of property

This is a much more common problem than you might think. I have spoken to countless people who have failed to make the revenue they had expected with the investment property they bought. They may have bought in the right location in the right phase of the property clock, but their problem was they did not get the right *type* of property that buyers in the area were in the market for.

One of the most important reasons I recommend buying houses as opposed to apartments is because each house on a street is somewhat distinguishable from the others. There is a useful amount of variance when comparing properties. Recall the problem of commercial or industrial properties, which are entirely unique even if they're right next door to each other. There are just too many variables to accurately derive an approximate value.

The opposite problem is when there are *too few* variables to distinguish one property from another. This is the case with an apartment, where every unit is the same as the one next to it. Suppose you are in a strong position and are ready to sell your unit, but at the same time, another owner down the hall is feeling financially distressed and wants to sell theirs. Because that seller is in a more desperate situation, they may be asking far less than what you're asking. Now, if you're a buyer and you see two indistinguishable pieces of property, but one is 20% cheaper than the other, which one are you going to buy?

Identifying the right type of property requires a thorough understanding of the demographics. How large are the households in the area? You don't want to buy a one-bedroom home if the neighbourhood is composed mostly of large families. What are their ages? You don't want the odd two-storey building if everyone around is well into retirement. What do residents do for fun? Do they like to host barbecues for friends in a big backyard, or have pool parties for the kids? Do they tend to have multiple vehicles and require a large enough garage to house them?

Sometimes, as an investor, you have to make somewhat broad generalisations. For example, I really like older people in a community. They tend to be house-proud. They like to garden and grow roses. They don't throw loud parties. They generally make fine neighbours. By and large, they have stable finances. And they don't move from place to place like young people often do. That's a recipe for a great tenant.

If you don't know who's moving in, there is no way you can know what they want. If you have not properly researched your market, your vacancy rates will reflect that.

Sin 6: Flipping

I come across this one way too often these days. There are a lot of people who just want to make a quick buck. And they've got a plan. They are going to renovate a house and turn around and sell it for a nice tidy profit.

That's the plan, anyway.

Let's begin with the most common mistake with this strategy: people almost never consider the true costs involved with buying, renovating and then selling. Take the fees, for starters. You've got stamp duty, which can run anywhere from $10,000 to $150,000 depending on the state where the property is located and the purchase price. There is the selling agent's commission, which is going to be somewhere between $20,000 and $100,000. There are advertising fees, due diligence fees, title transfer fees and registration fees. In short, there is a whole world of hidden transaction costs that most flippers just don't think through.

The barrier to go from one property to the next is high. It's not like selling shares.

Now, if you are a qualified builder and you run your own company and you have heaps of free time and access to surplus materials from your clients' construction projects, maybe you can find some success revamping a house and putting it back on the market. But that's a highly unusual situation.

And then, there's the problem of overcapitalising. You really need to research how you spend your money to try to add value. It's not a dollar-for-dollar return. It's critical to know which type of renovations increase value and which are unhelpful.

To begin with, it's necessary to know what the expectations are of a property like the one you're fixing up. I would suggest that the proper tool is a scalpel rather than a sledgehammer. Cosmetic renovations provide the best bang for the buck. That said, all too often, 'flippers' opt for large-scale improvements, which represents money that isn't well spent.

You don't need to put in a $20,000 ducted air conditioning system. If you're planning to sell the property, you could simply put in a reverse cycle split system – one in the living room, one in the master bedroom – for a third or a quarter of the price.

Neither do you need to put in a massive heated magnesium pool with automated cleaning when no one else in the neighbourhood has one. Sure, you might prefer a certain type of pool, but remember that you're not the buyer, you're the seller.

I don't recommend the strategy of flipping houses. Those shows you see on Netflix about couples getting rich rejuvenating homes is just entertainment. It's not real.

Sin 7: Managing the property yourself

I realise I've harped on this idea before, but it bears repeating: don't try to manage your properties yourself. It is a massive mistake.

Property management is not as simple as just going and collecting the rent. The tenancy legislation around the country is very complex. It's a minefield. If you don't know what you can and can't do, and if you don't understand all the processes, it will be a disaster. In fact, it puts you at risk. It puts your tenants at risk.

You don't want to be the person dealing with your tenants' calls every five minutes, or confronting them if they're a day late on rent, or repairing a blown light globe, or any other matter. You want to keep the tenant at arm's length. It's a business. You don't want to be the person micromanaging it.

What you want is someone you can rely on who is a qualified, experienced property manager. They know what they are doing because they do it day in and day out. They have databases of information. They know how to do appropriate background checks. Trust them to handle your investment because that's their business. It's not yours. You don't do your own dentistry, right?

Furthermore, if you have properties in different states, you have to realise that the laws are going to be unique for each one. It can get very confusing. And they all operate independently of one another. So, a notice period to evict a tenant in one state may be quite different than a neighbouring one. The processes you are required to go through may be completely different. It needs to be done correctly.

What happens if you fail to do all the necessary compliance checks? What if you miss a smoke detector, or a safety switch, or didn't realise that the pool is not in compliance? And now, what if something were to happen to a tenant as a result? You are the one who is liable. Leave it to a professional, and go enjoy your life.

Oh, and another thing ... don't try to find the cheapest property manager on the internet. It's true that you get what you pay for. There are always some dodgy new companies that pop up which are only in it for a minute. Maybe they've got one property manager with a thousand houses under management, and it's all done by automation. They don't have boots on the ground, they don't offer a personal touch, they're cheaper because they are not very good at what they do. If you call their phone, do you expect them to pick up?

This goes back to the chapter on using professionals. It's because they're good at their job and they have a passion for what they do. I want to use experts in their respective fields. I know that they will do a stellar job, and I won't be on holiday worrying about whether the pest inspector is going to miss finding the termites, or the building inspector is going to miss the mold, or the solicitor isn't going to do a basic search to find out you're buying in a flood zone.

When you cut corners to save a few bucks, you just end up paying for it down the road, and usually when you least expect it. Why not pay up front and sleep easy at night?

Chapter 9

When to buy your next investment property

You've invested in a property. Congratulations. Now what? How do you know when you're ready to buy *again*? What should you be thinking about when it comes to another investment property? While your initial purchase is your first step towards growing your wealth through property, knowing what to do next is just as important.

What's next?

This chapter is designed to provide a quick guide and some helpful info if you're wondering about purchasing a second property or more. You may be able to leverage your existing equity to keep doing what you're doing while having the peace of mind to know that you are not in danger of having to give up your nights out, or take on a second job, or worse, sell the property because you can no longer afford it.

So let's have a look at what's next in your property journey.

Check in with your goals

First and foremost, before you do anything, you need to check in with your financial and lifestyle goals.

What are your plans now and in the near future? Are you aiming to build a rental property portfolio over the next few years? Or do you want to live in your own home? These are important factors to consider when you're curious about entering the real estate market again as an investor.

Purchasing a second investment property offers a lot of wealth-creation opportunities, but that comes with a long-term mortgage commitment too, among other obligations. So, if you're thinking about searching the property market for a second time, just check to see how this aligns with your personal and financial goals.

Be mentally prepared

Acquiring your first property can be an eye-opening experience. You have to get used to the mortgage repayments, being a landlord, working with real estate agents, managing tenants, and so on.

While the second time around won't be completely new, you still have to be prepared. If you find that you're still coming to terms with everything and getting used to budgeting around loans, you're probably not quite ready yet. However, if everything is smooth sailing, you're ready to start looking again.

Make sure your first property has sufficient equity

Equity is the difference between the current market value of your first property and the outstanding balance of your loan on it. Your mortgage broker or lender can often allow you to access this equity to help you buy a second property by giving you finance against that amount.

If you have paid off a portion of your mortgage on the first investment property and/or its market value has increased, you may have sufficient equity you can draw upon to help you purchase an additional investment property.

Make sure you're financially secure

A second mortgage and a second investment property means double the costs to you, even with the extra rental income. However, if you're in a strong financial position, with a steady or increasing income and sufficient savings, you should have enough of a buffer to manage.

When you are financially secure, it means that if interest rates rise or any unexpected costs come up with any of your properties, you can comfortably afford them.

Make sure you are able to find the right property

Investing in real estate is always a risk, but there are a lot of opportunities to grow your wealth if you invest wisely in the right property.

Not all houses and apartments are the same, and knowing which option to buy can mean the difference between a profitable property portfolio and a mediocre one. While it can be time consuming, you should only consider purchasing another investment property if you have done enough research into the property market and identified suburbs and real estate that can offer you good returns on your investment.

Make sure you plan for land tax

In growing your portfolio and buying multiple real estate assets, you must prepare for the additional, often overlooked, taxes. Land tax is one such sneaky expense. It isn't something that is likely to be on your radar until you own several properties, or a really expensive second home, as it is not applicable to your principal place of residence.

Land tax is an item that investors need to be aware of as they consider a purchase within a state in which they already own property. It is essentially a space-based tax calculated on the total taxable value of an owner's freehold land – this figure excludes the dwelling value.

I mean, it's like the government is just printing money, right? They do *nothing* to earn that money but stick a bill in the mail. It's a cash grab. Not only do you pay stamp duty when you *buy* the item, but then they will get you going the other way, and charge you for *having* the item, and that's on top of council rates and any other holding costs associated with it. There, I got that off my chest.

So, anyway, every 12 months, the valuer general issues the annual land valuation for each property in your portfolio to determine if the value of your properties exceeds a certain minimum threshold. Each state makes its own rules as far as where that line is drawn, but if you're above it, you start paying on a sliding scale based on how much you own over that base amount.

It requires a reasonably complex equation to figure out what your number is going to be, as it varies based on whether you are an individual as opposed to a company, or a trust, or a super fund. Therefore, it's important to be mindful of how you are buying the property and make efforts to minimise your tax bill.

Consider this example from the Queensland Government website. Suppose you have an investment property valued at $680,000. The threshold in this state is $600,000, so you'd be just $80,000 above that amount. Based on the way that Queensland calculates that rate, you would be hit with a bill of $1,300 per year.

But as the value of your properties in the state rises and as your portfolio grows, so will your tax liability. That $1,300 bill can quickly blow up to $13,000. If you aren't ready to get stuck with a five-figure expenditure seemingly out of the blue, you would do well to plan ahead to minimise your tax penalty.

There are three reliable strategies you can use to minimise your land tax liability. This isn't a tax-avoidance scheme, but a course of action working within the tax laws, which a good accountant will go over with you in greater detail.

Buy across multiple states

The first strategy is simply to spread your holdings across multiple states to stay under the minimum threshold or at least in a significantly lower tax bracket. Queensland can't tax you for the beachfront house you have in New South Wales.

By diversifying your investments across state lines, you avoid accruing significant taxation.

Purchase as a different entity

Another way to avoid the tax collector is to diversify the way in which you own properties within a given state. If you own multiple expensive properties as an individual, you are likely to get stuck writing a significant cheque. But if you own one property in your name and another as part of a trust, and yet another is held in a super fund, each is considered separate from the other. As a result, they are each assessed individually at given rates, and *not* added together when calculating the value of your holdings.

Purchase with another buyer

The third method to minimise your tax penalty is to buy under someone else's name. I don't mean just *anyone's* name. This is commonly done under a spouse's name. The deed is going to be in that person's name, so you obviously want to use the most trusted person in your life. And assuming that person does not have a significant amount of assets, you will have managed to spread your holdings horizontally, rather than stack them vertically, so to speak.

Sharing the wealth in this manner will keep you under the threshold, or at least far lower than you would have been had you piled it all up yourself.

~

As you can see, there are ways that are completely legitimate to reduce your land tax, but that is something a lot of people overlook, as it is not well-publicised. It isn't like the government is going to advertise that sort of advice.

I always recommend that people seek proper independent advice from a qualified accountant or financial planner about methods or ways to minimise land tax. You want to work with someone who can find the right personalised method for your unique situation.

Chapter 10

How to pay off your mortgage in half the time

If you have a 30-year mortgage, you may feel like you'll be paying off your loan for the better part of your life. Having this massive debt lingering over your head for such a long time can prevent you from enjoying early retirement or taking your dream holiday. So, the sooner you get rid of your home mortgage, the better off you'll be down the track.

Because property is often both a long-term investment as well as a huge expenditure, a lack of a solid plan will likely impact your lifestyle in a significant way.

So, how do you pay off your home loan quickly?

While there is no *one size fits all* solution, I've got five useful tips to help you meet your goals and pay off your home loan sooner. Keep in mind, however, this is simply general information and *not* financial advice. It doesn't take into account your specific personal circumstances and should only be used as a guide.

Five helpful tips to pay off your mortgage in half the time

Your home loan is probably the biggest investment you'll make and it's usually the debt you would like to get off your back as quickly as you can.

While most mortgages come with a 30-year term, that doesn't mean you *must* have it for that long. These five helpful tips can help you get ahead on your loan to allow you to potentially save yourself a significant amount of money on interest charges.

Tip 1: Go a little above and beyond each month

Home ownership is the Great Aussie Dream. Securing your main residence as early as possible can help you build a strong foundation for your property investment strategy towards achieving your financial freedom.

I talk to homebuyers every day, many of whom are either buying for their first or their second home, and they've got some very long-term mortgages, usually about 30 years. And they're of course thinking of eventual retirement, but they know that it's impossible until they pay off that mortgage. You can't just stop bringing in money when you've got loan payments to make. So, I make it a priority to have them focus on paying off that primary residence right away. You need to own that outright because it is not tax deductible. Once you do pay off that mortgage, there are some really great advantages that ensue.

Once you own the roof over your head, you begin accruing equity. That money can be reinvested. And with an investment property, the interest on the loan *is* tax deductible.

So, with that purpose in mind, here's a tip: pay a little *extra* off your home loan each month or make more frequent payments to shorten your mortgage time. You'll be surprised how much this compounds. Just check to ensure there are no penalties involved with paying off your mortgage sooner.

Here is an example:

> Mr Warren decides to contribute an additional $400 per month on top of his required $2,400 monthly home loan repayment. So, he's now paying $2,800 each month.
>
> Over the span of 12 months, he pays $33,600, which is roughly equivalent to two additional months' worth of payments each year. This simple strategy will shave about six years and three months off Mr Warren's 30-year loan term and will save him around $67,500 in interest.

By going a little above and beyond each month, Mr Warren has saved more than six years of making payments and pocketed nearly $70,000.

Tip 2: Use equity to build your property portfolio

If you have already paid off some of your main home loan, you have already started building equity. Equity is simply the difference between the current value of your property and the amount left on your mortgage. When set up correctly, this amount can be used to finance the purchase of additional property.

How many properties? Well, that's really up to you. It depends on your personal wants and needs. For the average family committed to modest spending, I recommend purchasing five investment properties. It sounds like a lot, but it's actually not when you get right down to it. After all, you're probably not buying those five properties at once, you're doing it over a period of time.

The key is to hold on to those properties as you buy them. And if you buy the right types of houses in well-located areas, it's just a matter of letting capital growth do its thing. And then you build your portfolio just using the equity from the properties you acquire. You may be negatively or neutrally geared at first, but that will change over time as the rent goes up and up.

Eventually, the entire portfolio ends up being positively geared, which starts bringing in cashflow, which makes holding the assets very easy.

If you have assets that don't cost anything, and which are earning disposable income, it's quite easy to hold onto them. So, it's just a matter of building and maintaining that portfolio. Don't try to flip your properties in an attempt to make a quick buck, just hold on and wait for the capital growth. And if you hang on for 10 or 15 years, they're likely to double or triple in value.

Here is a sample scenario of building your portfolio through equity:

> Mrs Park has a property that's worth $600,000 on which she still owes $250,000. That means she now has a home equity amount of $350,000, which she can use to purchase one or two additional properties. This equity can help build her portfolio and leverage it as a way to earn more by renting the properties out to cover costs.

Tip 3: Set up your bank accounts for maximum benefit

Unless you have an accountant with whom you discuss financial matters or have pursued an education in the field, you are probably operating like most homebuyers, with a shallow understanding of the various types of financial options at your disposal.

A home loan offset account may not even be on your radar, but it should be. It allows you to offset or reduce the interest charged on your mortgage. This is basically a transaction account attached to your home loan, with which you can make deposits or withdraw funds as you would with a regular transaction account.

Essentially, when the lender calculates your monthly interest repayments, they will subtract any money you hold in the offset account from the home loan balance and then determine the interest repayment.

A lot of folks set up a home loan, obviously for their home, and then establish a savings account into which all their money is deposited on a monthly basis. And the loan repayment is drawn from that account and put towards the home loan. But here's the thing, if they had set up an offset account, any money deposited in it offsets the interest charged on the mortgage.

So, if you look at your savings account, you might be getting 0.1% or maybe 0.2% interest, and of course, you report that to the government, which then taxes you on that interest! And this is just a course of action that a lot of people pursue without questioning it.

Bottom line: setting up an offset account can significantly reduce your monthly interest costs, allowing you to contribute more of your regular payments towards paying down the loan principal. This, in turn, can help you pay off your mortgage sooner.

Tip 4: Help your assets grow

Property values tend to grow over time. Market conditions set that schedule. That said, there are actions you can take to manufacture growth.

Cosmetic renovations are an easy and affordable way you can increase your existing property value. You could also consider a modernised kitchen, refreshing the paintwork, replacing the carpets or basic landscaping, which will make a huge difference in the home value. These value-adding options should definitely be considered, especially if you are planning to sell within the next few years. But they also will increase rental income in the meantime, and can get you positively geared quicker than you might have planned, allowing you to increase your cashflow.

Tip 5: Sell your investments

If you sell one or two investment properties after 10 to 15 years, you'll often find that the capital value has increased significantly. Keep in mind that prices can fluctuate, so if you are planning to sell a property, wait until the market is favourable so as to maximise your gains.

Then, you can either take those gains to pay off a good portion of your outstanding mortgage balance or even eliminate the mortgage altogether.

Once you have your main residence and five properties in your investment portfolio, and you've held onto them for enough time, you can cherry pick which ones to sell and which ones to keep hanging onto. If you sell three of them, you will create enough revenue to completely pay off the loan balances and any additional costs, leaving you free and clear of debt on your main residence, *plus* two additional properties, which are bringing in a passive income.

There's an added benefit to this, and that's inflation. That may sound counterintuitive, but as a landlord, rising prices means the rent you charge can be increased. Inflation rises every year, and every year rents go up accordingly.

But if you're not in this position, think about what that means. Consider a mum and dad who are now 70 years old, and have retired with, let's be generous, $300,000 in their super fund. Their retirement plan is to draw on that each year to cover living expenses. And as they're drawing that down, the cost of living is simultaneously going up. It's a lose–lose situation in which they're depleting their funds at the same time that the money they do have just doesn't buy what it used to. Stressful, right? Time to adjust that retirement plan, right?

That's the scenario I want to help you avoid. The goal is to become unencumbered by debt, with no mortgage hanging over your head, while also bringing in a passive income every month of your life, which will provide you the stability you need for retirement (*whatever* that means for you).

But getting there doesn't just *happen*. You have to plan it and you have to execute it properly. And then, you have to stick with it. That's the hard part. There's something in human nature that drives us to action even when the smart decision is to simply do nothing.

If you're a goalkeeper on a penalty kick, what are you going to do? Are you going to dive left or right, or are you going to just hold your ground and be prepared for a direct shot? It's natural to dive one way or the other, but sometimes the best strategy is to just play the centre of the goal.

Are you ready to move towards financial freedom?

Paying off your home loan sooner can be a positive move towards financial freedom, but doing so involves planning your investment strategies as early as possible. This way, you can leave more cash in your pocket over time and live with fewer worries, so that you are able to enjoy the fruits of your labour.

Remember, this is just *general* information. As always, speak to your financial advisor to get advice that's tailored to your specific circumstances.

Here's an example of how leveraging into real estate could help reduce the time it takes to pay off a home loan from 30 years to 15.

> Mum and Dad, roughly 40 years old, own one property with a 30-year loan term, owing $600,000 (for the sake of simplicity, this scenario is based on *interest-only* loans).
>
> They are worried that they are going to be 70 years old before they pay off their mortgage and finally own their home.

Current situation

Main residence

Home loan	$600,000
Property value	$1,200,000

Solution

Value × 80%	$960,000
Available equity	$360,000

Strategy

Apply for a top-up loan (or equity release loan) for $260,000; these funds can be used to purchase two investment properties (2 × $100,000 deposits + costs of $30,000 each)

Top-up loan	$260,000

Investment property 1

Investment loan A	$400,000
Purchase price	$500,000

Investment property 2

Investment loan B	$400,000
Purchase price	$500,000

Future state

Hold onto the assets for 15 years paying interest only and paying any surplus funds into the home mortgage or into an offset account.

Main residence

Home loan	$600,000
Top-up loan	$260,000
Property value	$2,400,000

Investment property 1

Investment loan A	$400,000
Property value	$1,000,000

Investment property 2

Investment loan B	$400,000
Property value	$1,000,000

The next step is to sell the investment portfolio and eliminate all non-deductible main residence debt.

Sale amount	$2,000,000
Selling agent commission	$50,000
Funds available from the sale	$1,950,000

Loans to pay down

Home loan	$600,000	
Investment loan A	$400,000	
Investment loan B	$400,000	
Top-up loan	$260,000	
Less total Loans		$1,660,000
Minus CGT*		$200,250
Remaining balance after tax		$89,750

* Refer to the CGT calculations overleaf.

These are very basic calculations and not all costs or depreciation have been taken into consideration. All debts have now been repaid and the main residence is unencumbered; the clients in this example would be just 55 years old.

They now need to look at generating a passive income. If they repeat the same strategy, this time with five investments, in another

15 years, they can sell three and keep the others for a passive income with which to support their lifestyle.

Capital gains tax (CGT) calculations

If you make a profit from the sale of an investment property, you will most likely need to pay CGT – there are some factors to consider, such as how the property was originally purchased (for example, individually, or via a company or trust structure).

The profit will be the difference between what you purchased the property for and the sale price. The profit amount will then be added to your assessable income and taxed at the applicable rate.

CGT calculation for example above

$2,000,000 (the capital proceeds) minus $1,110,000
(the cost base, made up of: purchase costs + stamp duty
+ conveyancing fees + agent's commission) = $890,000
× 50% CGT discount = $445,000 × income tax rate (45%)
= $200,250 (approx. tax payable)

Generally, a capital gain is eligible for the CGT discount if you are an Australian resident, and you owned the asset for at least 12 months.

Warning: You should seek professional advice if you need an accurate estimate for tax purposes.

Final thoughts

The best time to invest in property was *yesterday*. But good news: the next-best time is *today*. As I look back on that first house that I purchased, at 20 years young, I can trace my current success back to that day, sitting down at the bank and signing my name on the dotted line.

There is no investment quite like residential real estate, and the sooner you get a piece of it, the sooner it will begin rewarding your decision with a passive income. And as you are no doubt now aware, passive income is the only way off the treadmill of a regular job. Unless you want to work until you die, you've got to find a way to, as Warren Buffett put it, 'make money while you sleep'.

Nothing is as stable over time as property. Nobody *needs* shares in the market but everyone needs a roof over their head. Furthermore, demand outpaces supply, as no one is going to build a housing estate just to let it sit empty until the population eventually grows and catches up. And of course, scarcity drives up prices. If you own property, that means the value is rising; if you are paying to live in someone else's place, it means your costs are rising.

Commercial property can be part of a balanced portfolio but is not as reliable as residential property for consistent returns. Houses can be measured much more systematically, and are comparable like apples to apples, whereas commercial or industrial properties can each be unique in their own way even if they're right next door to each other.

Putting together a professional, reliable team will ensure there's little chance of your deal falling over. That all begins with finding the right buyer's agent, who will hold your hand throughout the process and will get you to the finish line. Because this is my area of expertise, I can tell you how critical it is to get this member of your team right, because if you don't, it's going to affect everything else. It's like a goalkeeper: if you've got a good one, you'll be competitive regardless of the rest of the team; but if you've got a lousy one, it doesn't matter who else you've got, you're going to be in trouble.

It also means working with the right accountant, who will be proactive in finding you every tax advantage; the right mortgage broker, who you want to be independent and have allegiances with you first, in addition to the bank; building and pest inspectors who don't cut corners and who do your due diligence for you; a reliable conveyancer, who will basically manage the relationship between you and the seller until settlement; a reputable insurer, who will combine a high level of service with a high level of coverage; and for a wide variety of reasons, an experienced property manager, because that is not a job for you to be doing yourself.

Of course, you can have an all-star team of professionals in your corner, but if you're buying in the wrong location, it's all moot anyway. The pillars I outlined are essential in finding the ideal location to buy: what phase is the property cycle in? Is the market peaking? Is it waning? Is it bottoming out? You want the quickest return on your investment, so you want to find a location that's on the upswing.

What does the data tell you? For instance, what is the vacancy rental rate? Is your property going to be unoccupied for long stretches of time? How about historical capital growth?

Is investment dwindling over time or growing? What is the average number of days on market for a property in the area? Do homes get bought up quickly or do they sit there?

What is going to drive growth and attract new residents? Are there infrastructure deals in the works? A new hospital or university coming in? Large-scale investments require extensive research and due diligence. If major companies have decided to locate in the area, you can bet they've done their homework.

What's the community composed of? Who lives there? Is it a neighbourhood of ageing retirees? Growing families? Young singles? Does the particular property you're looking at fit with what the target demographic wants? You don't want to buy a one-bedroom house with a tiny yard in an area where everyone has at least three children and a dog.

And finally, what is your cashflow? Remember, you got into this deal to make money. Real estate investing needs to be treated like a business, rather than a hobby. It's critical to forecast your projected income and weigh that against all the related expenses. If the numbers don't add up, you need to walk away.

The buying process can be intimidating if you haven't been through it before. For that matter, it can be intimidating even if you've been through it several times. I've provided you with enough information in this book, however, to make your journey go a little smoother.

A smooth buying process begins with determining your expectations and it requires planning far ahead into the future, 10, 20 or maybe 30 years down the road. It requires keeping a 'cushion' in the bank just in case, considering all your available loan options, determining if a principal or interest-only loan is your best option, and bearing in mind that because interest rates fluctuate over time, you should factor in at least two to three points above where you're currently at just as a precaution. Finally, it necessitates making sure you are selecting the ideal property.

Having found the ideal property, how do you know what a fair price is? And how do you get the seller to agree to it? Fair market value can only be determined by using a comparative market analysis. And it's not only the seller's job to figure out what the market is, it's also up to the buyer to know what the property is worth, which will be invaluable when it comes time to negotiate the price.

A comparative market analysis involves studying at least three similar properties that have been sold, not just listed. Your comparable properties need to be relatively nearby, within about five kilometres. And they need to have been recently sold, within six months' time.

As you negotiate from there, you will want to know how long those comparables were on the market. Was it hot or cold? Are there other factors that might make the properties less comparable? Maybe a nearby home sold for the same price but is two bedrooms larger and has a pool. Or maybe it was sold to a family member for a discounted price. Or maybe the owner died and the heirs just wanted to be done with the estate with as little fuss as possible. On the other hand, maybe the buyers overpaid to buy back a home that they had grown up in. It's important to make sure your comparables *are* actually comparable.

As with any investment, there are major problems you want to avoid. I have identified the seven that are the most deadly mistakes you can make. The most common problem is proximity. There's nothing that says your investment has to be located near you. There's an inherent bias people have to their own communities. The advice they're getting is most likely from the people in their communities and is well intentioned, but it's important to acknowledge that such information is not objective or independent. Then, there's the idea that investing locally would be convenient, but bear in mind, you don't need to be checking in on it.

The second deadly sin is getting emotionally connected to a property. Buyers often make the mistake of picturing themselves living in the home rather than distancing themselves and keeping a more rational mindset about the property.

Treating the purchase as a tax strategy as opposed to a long-term investment is dangerous, and it's the third sin. Tax minimisation ought to be considered a bonus in your investment plan, not the basis of it.

Ignoring the property cycle is the fourth deadly sin, and is a major no-no. It's always the right time to buy somewhere, and it's always the wrong time to buy somewhere else. Knowing when to buy is critical.

Fifth in the list of deadly property investment sins is buying the wrong type of property. Just because you've found the right neighbourhood at the right time doesn't mean you've found the right property. If you acquire a five-bedroom house spread across three floors in an area overflowing with retirees, good luck finding a tenant.

Sixth, avoid trying to flip a property. Renovations rarely provide the desired return on investment. It's generally not a dollar-for-dollar return. There are also a lot of fees involved – listing fees, due diligence fees, title transfer fees, registration fees – which people tend to overlook. There are too many hidden transactional costs to make the flipping strategy viable.

And finally, the seventh deadly sin: managing the property yourself. It's hard to think of a worse idea. Your life will be so much easier knowing that a reliable property manager is on the job. Consider it a transaction cost if it helps, just build it right into the price. If you're still considering taking the role of property manager in your investment, I urge you to do yourself a favour and go back and reread that section.

The guidance I've provided in these pages is not only designed to help you in your first investment, because a property investment should not be undertaken as a series of one-off transactions but rather as a singular, long-term strategy in which each purchase is a tactical step towards an ultimate goal. This being the case, I've included a chapter on buying your next property.

When you're ready to make the leap to a second or subsequent investment property, you need to first check in with your goals. Where are you trying to get financially and what type of lifestyle do you want to enjoy? What are your plans for the near future? Do you own your home or are you looking to buy? A second investment property creates an abundance of wealth-building opportunities but also presents a variety of obligations, so you need to ensure your goals are aligned with any purchasing decision.

Next, you need to be sure you're up for the experience both mentally and emotionally. Generally, once you've already been through the buying process, it gets easier, but not always. Your first go-round may have been smooth sailing due to market conditions at the time. But the winds can and do shift, and your next foray could be into a hostile environment in which homes go off the market in just three days, or are auctioned off far above the market value, or simply aren't available. Are you in a peaceful state of mind so you can coolly handle such adverse conditions?

You also want to be certain that your first property has attained sufficient equity before venturing out on a second. The last thing you want is to find yourself struggling to pay off two properties at once. But if you've established enough equity in the first property, your mortgage broker will allow you to draw upon that to get into a second.

On a similar note, and this should go without saying, you need to be financially secure. Are you prepared if interest rates should suddenly rise or if there's an unexpected expenditure on your first property that requires fixing? Do you have sufficient income or savings to create a buffer against an emergency cost?

Are you buying simply because you have the equity to do so, or have you found the ideal property and are in a strong financial position? A mediocre investment will set you back and put you behind on your long-term goals. It benefits you to take the time to find the right property rather than buying just for the sake of quickly adding to your portfolio. There's no excuse for shortcutting your due diligence. And this is where a buyer's agent can be tremendously useful.

Yet another consideration to bear in mind as you build your portfolio is hidden costs. A crucial and potentially costly one that buyers often overlook is land tax. This sneaky expense will creep up on you as your properties accumulate value.

There are ways to mitigate that expense, and I have provided some strategies to do so. The first, of course, is to spread your holdings across multiple states to avoid the line at which tax penalties begin to kick in. By diversifying your investments across state lines, you dodge significant taxation.

Another way to get around the hit to your bank account is to purchase in different entities. You may own one property in your name and another as part of a trust or super fund, yet each is considered a separate holding and assessed individually at given rates.

You can also minimise your burden by buying under the name of your spouse, a parent or an adult child, someone close enough to you that you trust having the deed in their name. This is a way to spread your holdings horizontally as opposed to stacking them vertically. Your financial planner or accountant can tailor to your own unique situation a personalised method to reduce your tax liability.

If you've picked up this book, it's probably because you're ready to begin investing in property or want to develop a strategy to improve your existing portfolio. Whatever your personal situation, I hope the information I've provided will serve as a helpful guide you will reference like a playbook. To that end, I've closed with five essential tips to pay off your home loan faster, because the sooner you do that, the closer you are to your ultimate goals in retirement.

First and foremost, work on a plan to pay off your main residence. Live the Great Aussie Dream. This is the foundation of a solid strategy and the first step towards financial freedom.

Once you've established enough equity, it's time to take a small leap and begin leveraging that equity towards an investment property that will begin bringing in passive income.

Third is something that many investors overlook and that's staying on top of your bank accounts and ensuring they're always set up in your best financial interest. For example, a home loan offset account may allow you to reduce the interest charged on your mortgage. The account is attached to your home loan and allows you to make deposits and withdrawals just as you would with a regular transaction account, but when the lender calculates your monthly interest repayments they'll subtract any money you hold in the offset account from the home loan balance and, crucially, then determine the interest repayment.

And this is why a proactive accountant is so important. They don't sit back and put your financial future on autopilot. Instead, they're constantly on the lookout for any advantages in the tax code they can find for you.

My fourth tip is to give your assets the time they need to grow – but if you can speed up the schedule, by all means do so. Accelerated growth might come in the form of cosmetic renovations, which will not only increase the value of the property in the long run but will allow you to demand higher rents in the short term. Anything that adds to cashflow gets you that much closer to your next investment purchase.

Eventually, your investments will bear fruit and that's when you sell. There will come a point at which the return on your investment has paid dividends and is worth cashing in on, so that you can use the profits to either pay off your own mortgage or reinject into a property that has become lucrative because of where it's at on the property clock.

Because of the many transaction costs involved, you just can't divest and reinvest frequently. Additionally, it takes several years for a property to increase enough in value that it becomes ripe for selling. But when your portfolio has grown to five properties, you can cherry pick which to hold and which to sell.

Five investment properties, consider that a reasonable goal. If you can manage that, and I've given you the tools to do so, you will be able to rely on a passive income for the rest of your life, allowing you to enjoy the recreation and leisure that a comfortable lifestyle affords. The sooner you take the first step, the sooner you'll complete the journey. It's my journey, too, and it's been my pleasure to see you on the path.